The preservation of liberty is
a point equally nice with the
preservation of a ladies chastity;
the first assaults are to be repelled with the utmost fortitude.
A maidenhead, a fort, or a constitution that begins to capitulate
will soon surrender.

"Portius,"
*O Liberty, Thou Goddess
Heavenly Bright*
(New York, 1732)

Liberty and
Authority

Generously Donated to

The Frederick Douglass Institute

By Professor Jesse Moore

Fall 2000

Liberty and Authority

EARLY AMERICAN
POLITICAL IDEOLOGY
1689-1763

BY

Lawrence H. Leder

The Norton Library

W·W·NORTON & COMPANY·INC·

NEW YORK

COPYRIGHT © 1968 BY LAWRENCE H. LEDER

First published in the Norton Library 1976
by arrangement with Quadrangle Books

ALL RIGHTS RESERVED
Published simultaneously in Canada
by George J. McLeod Limited, Toronto

Library of Congress Cataloging in Publication Data
Leder, Lawrence H.
    Liberty and authority.
    (The Norton Library)
    Reprint of the ed. published by Quadrangle Books,
Chicago.
    Includes bibliographical references and index.
    1. Political science—History—United States. I. Ti-
tle.
[JA84.U5L37 1976]   320.5'0973   75-31777
ISBN 0-393-00800-2

Printed in the United States of America
1 2 3 4 5 6 7 8 9 0

For Bernice

ACKNOWLEDGMENTS

IN PREPARING any book a variety of debts are incurred, and this work is no exception. The staffs of many libraries have gone out of their way to provide courteous and expert help and thereby have facilitated my research. Not least among these was the staff at my own institution, Louisiana State University in New Orleans, whose forbearance in my countless negotiations for inter-library loans was exemplary.

Dr. Lester C. Cappon and the staff of the Institute of Early American History and Culture, Williamsburg, Virginia, provided me with microfilmed newspapers on an almost split-second schedule. Miss Doris L. Payne of the University of Washington Library in Seattle made available several important microfilmed newspapers which do not ordinarily circulate. To Miss Geraldine Beard of the New York Historical Society, I am indebted for providing runs of several important newspapers and for otherwise aiding me in research over the years. The staffs of the Boston Atheneum and the Massachusetts Historical Society also offered their traditional courteous service.

Finally, I wish to express my gratitude to the Louisiana State University Research Council for a grant-in-aid during the summer of 1963 which made possible the preliminary research on this book and to the American Council of Learned Societies for a grant-in-aid during the summer of 1964 which enabled me to complete much of the investigation necessary. I am also indebted to the Henry E. Huntington Library and Art Gallery for a grant-in-aid which circumstances prevented me from using in the summer of 1965. I am grateful to the Huntington organization for permission to utilize, in Chapter One of this book, material which appeared in my article in the *Huntington Library Quarterly,* "The Role of Newspapers in Early America: 'In Defense of Their Own Liberty.' "

My thanks go also to those who typed the manuscript of this book in its several versions—Mrs. Eva Carr and Mrs. Gloria Savage. To my wife and children who bore with me during the dark and hopefully bright moments of authorship and who spurred me on to complete the task, my deepest appreciation. The responsibility for what follows is solely mine.

L. H. L.

New Orleans, 1968

INTRODUCTION

AN ASTUTE British observer in 1763 evaluated the Anglo-American situation in these words: "The House of Commons has resolved . . . that the colonies have no constitution, but that the mode of government in each of them depends upon the good pleasure of the King, as expressed in his commission and instructions to the governor. The colonists, however, consider themselves as entitled to a greater measure of liberty than is enjoyed by the people of England, because of their quitting their native country to make settlements for the advantage of Great Britain in the wilds of America. Hence the perpetual struggle in every colony between privilege and prerogative."[1]

This perpetual struggle forms the core of this book, at least insofar as Americans sought to justify in theory what they demanded in practice during the years from the Glorious Revolution of 1688–1689 to the end of the French and Indian War in 1763. There have been many examinations of the practical demands, but almost nothing has been written about the political theory that emerged to support them. This theory is in itself important and, when set against the onrushing American Revolution, provides a key to understanding why loyal colonials found it necessary to become rebellious Americans in the short span of thirteen years.

The aspects of theory which require examination are complex. Did Americans develop an understanding of man's presocial existence or a concept of the origin of government? How did American conceptions of these matters correspond with ideas held in England? What relationship had Americans worked out between church and state, and how did this affect their view of the state's role? To what extent did they understand the meaning and function of constitutionalism in general and of the British constitution in particular? Were Americans able to reach any universal conclusions about the nature of their own constitutions, and if so, what effects did these estimates have upon efforts at colonial unity before 1763 and the colonial response to increased British pressure afterward?

Why, indeed, was Thomas Jefferson in 1776 forced to resort to "self-evident" truths in explaining the American position when Americans for a century had been hailing the rights of Englishmen as the ultimate bastion of liberty? Did the colonials really understand the rights and liberty of which they had spoken so glibly, or had they merely been trumpeting slogans without examining their content? In the answers to these questions may also be found suggestions as to why the British backed away so quickly from their initial attempts at taxation and the use of admiralty court procedures, as well as an explanation of why Americans appeared so defenseless against later efforts at imperial regulation and control.

The whole of eighteenth-century American politics has only recently been explored in detail. While general works that deal with the entire period are few, those that concern themselves with political thought are even rarer. Clinton P. Rossiter's *Seedtime of the Republic,* in treating the political thought of this period, focuses upon six intellectual giants—Thomas Hooker, Roger Williams, John Wise, Jonathan Mayhew, Richard Bland, and Benjamin Franklin.[2] As a consequence of this selectivity, the book begs a basic question—whether the colonials at large *were* searching for a republic, and further, whether these leaders truly reflected popular attitudes in their own day.

A preliminary probe into the mystery was provided by Max

Savelle's *Seeds of Liberty,* but he examined the whole pano-
rama of colonial thought and could thus devote only limited
attention to political theory.[3] Trevor Colbourn, in his *The
Lamp of Experience,* has ably traced the origin of American
ideas from the historical literature read by colonials, but once
again—were these ideas universally held, or did they belong
to an exclusive *avant-garde* leadership?[4] To date there has
been only one major effort to penetrate the ideas held by
Americans in general, and that for only a limited period.
Bernard Bailyn's introduction to his *Pamphlets of the American
Revolution* gives us an exhaustive analysis of the political
theory current from 1750 to 1763.[5]

Even though Bailyn has not yet developed an analysis of
political thought in the whole three-quarters of a century before
1763, he has recognized its importance. In an essay reviewing
the summary work of the imperial school of historians, he
wrote: "What is missing . . . on the background and origin
of the Revolution are politics and ideology." The American
Revolution, he contended, "was above all else an ideological
revolution, and it is in ideological terms essentially that its
origination is comprehensible. A complex tradition of ideas,
fused into a coherent whole largely in the very early years
of the eighteenth century, came into conjunction with a peculiar structure of informal politics in America to create, already
by mid-century, a latently revolutionary situation."[6] What
must be defined, however, was the way in which this situation
was "latently revolutionary."

But the basic concept that there was a political ideology is
not new. Merrill Jensen, in a commentary written in 1958 for
a new edition of Randolph G. Adams' *Political Ideas of the
American Revolution,* sought to sketch the ideological background and suggest its importance. "The Americans who debated the nature and foundations of their rights and privileges
with the mother country after 1763," wrote Jensen, "were
for the most part not dealing with new ideas. What they were

doing was reforming and reiterating ideas which had been a part of their English heritage, and to which they had appealed over and over again in the course of a century and a half. . . . They had been known and used in one way or another throughout the course of American colonial political history. Only the context in which these theories were used, and the intensity with which they were stated, were new in the years between 1763 and 1776."

It was beyond the scope of Jensen's commentary to explore this thought in any detail. And since he was suggestive rather than definitive in his statements, he naturally arrived at some conclusions whose validity he could not test, and which have not since been critically examined. That "the Americans knew what the guarantee of the rights of Englishmen meant," and that "the rights of colonial legislatures and legislators and of individuals as colonists and Englishmen were thus firmly fixed in American minds long before the crucial debate began with the mother country in the years after 1763" are convenient and comfortable assumptions.[7]

Out of such assumptions readily emerges the simplistic and pro-American idea that the English were pigheaded and stubborn, traitors to their own heritage, perhaps even corrupt when they rejected the validity of the American position after 1763. But was the situation as clear and simple as that view would imply? Can all the guilt be placed on one side of the Atlantic? Finding answers to these questions poses difficulties of method. Rossiter's analysis of the concepts held by six great intellectuals in his *Seedtime of the Republic* is a traditional approach, but it reinforces the patriotic bias and has other limitations. It certainly is no guarantee of an understanding of American thought in its broadest sense. Were these men abreast of the people, or ahead of them? If they had outdistanced their age, how far ahead had they gone? Or, more precisely, by what criteria can we designate them as leaders in their own day? Since the traditional approach leaves these questions unanswered, we remain uncertain about the political thought shared by American society at large. To try to remove this uncertainty, I have shifted the approach. I have examined all materials in print—newspapers, magazines, books, broadsides, pamphlets, sermons, brochures, and so forth—which met two conditions: first, that they issued from American presses; and second, that they were written by Americans in the years from 1689 to 1763. By examining both what Americans wrote and what they read, I have attempted to establish the broadest kind of base for some conclusions about the political thought that was shared as a common colonial heritage in the years before the Anglo-American relationship was seriously disturbed by the conscious effort of the British to reshape the empire.

This method, I appreciate, is also limited in its effectiveness. We cannot really determine precisely the total number of readers of any given essay or book. Nor can we be certain of the reader's comprehension. We do know that the literacy rate in the American colonies was exceptionally high and that materials such as newspaper essays and brochures and pamphlets were frequently read aloud in public gatherings. We can therefore assume that ideas in print had a fairly wide circulation. Results based upon such an assumption cannot of course be conclusive. But the findings do provide an understanding of colonial political thought based upon as broad a collection of evidence as the historian can now accumulate for so remote a period.

Because my concern has been with the ideas themselves, I have given but cursory attention to the often petty quarrels from which great principles sometimes emerged. The political history of these years admittedly stands in need of fresh investigation and fresh synthesis, but until someone chooses to perform that task, Herbert Levi Osgood's monumental four volumes, *The American Colonies in the Eighteenth Century,* must suffice for background material.[8] Neither have I been particularly concerned with the origin of the ideas expressed by Americans. Others have done significant work in this area, particularly Caroline Robbins in *The Eighteenth-Century Commonwealthman*[9] and Trevor Colbourn in *The Lamp of Experience*.[10] My purpose, to borrow a phrase from Daniel Boorstin, has been to try to recapture the ideas of the eighteenth century rather than perform an autopsy on them.[11] If I have had any success in this, perhaps a new approach can eventually be made toward the problem of the American Revolution itself.

In quoting from eighteenth-century materials, I have eliminated many peculiarities of style which can only serve to annoy a modern reader. Thus, eighteenth-century variants in capitalization, spelling, and punctuation have been silently regularized by modern standards. In none of these changes have I knowingly interfered with the original meaning or emphasis of the authors quoted.

A brief word concerning the dating of newspapers which I have cited: in each instance the date is given precisely as it appeared on the masthead. For newspapers published before 1752 during the dates January 1 to March 24, this frequently means the use of a double year (e.g., March 1, 1724/5). England remained on the Julian Calendar until 1752, while much of Europe had used the Gregorian Calendar since 1582. Not only did this mean an actual difference in the numbering of days of the month between the Continent and England (and therefore her colonies), but it also meant that England legally followed the Julian practice of starting the New Year on Annunciation Day, March 25. This complication was resolved by the custom after 1670 of citing both the old and new years for any date between January 1 and March 24. Thus the first year given is the legal year and the second is the actual one. Further discussion of this can be found conveniently in Oscar Handlin, *et al., Harvard Guide to American History* (Cambridge, Mass., 1960), pp. 91–93.

CONTENTS

ACKNOWLEDGMENTS 7

INTRODUCTION 9

I. *The Role of the Press* 19

II. *The State of Nature and the Origin of Government* 37

III. *Religion and the State* 61

IV. *Constitutional Theory and the British Constitution* 79

V. *The Colonial Constitutions* 95

VI. *Rights and Liberties* 118

VII. *The Concept of Empire: A Fatal Flaw* 131

VIII. *The Ideological Discontinuity* 140

NOTES 147

BIBLIOGRAPHICAL NOTE 161

INDEX 163

Liberty and
Authority

I
The Role of the Press

IT HAS often been assumed that eighteenth-century Americans' views of society, government, and liberty were sharply different from those of their contemporaries in Britain or on the European continent. Thomas Paine once phrased it succinctly: "In the commencement of a revolution, those men (the distortedly debased men who make up the European mob) are rather the followers of the *camp* than of the *standard* of liberty, and have yet to be instructed how to reverence it." A recent study has illustrated the sharp differences in mob understanding during the Stamp Act Crisis in New York, the assault on the Bastille in Paris, and the Lord George Gordon Riots in London.[1]

The contrast clearly exists, but to what is it due? Paine understood the situation: the Americans reverenced liberty. To them it was more than a phrase to be shouted from the ramparts; it had a meaning and substance all its own. This was certainly the result of the extended experience of local self-government in the colonies and of the lack of feudal hierarchies and social rigidities in America, but still another element was involved.

Throughout the eighteenth century, Americans had freely discussed the basic elements of political theory, sometimes with sharp insight and sometimes naively. Their discussions had evolved a working hypothesis, a viable definition of government which satisfied their immediate needs until 1763. From that time forward, events seemed to violate the basic precepts of their theory, and they were forced to re-evaluate their own framework. In the process they retained some of the earlier theory, more sharply defined other aspects of it, and added some new ideas.

But American goals remained unchanged. For three-quarters of a century these had been expounded in pamphlets, broadsides, magazines, and newspapers; ministers had spelled them out in sermons. Armed with these commonly understood goals, and supported by broad theoretical justifications, Americans confidently entered the struggle with Britain over the meaning and extent of liberty. A rude awakening awaited them, but the colonists would hardly have begun the conflict had they lacked confidence in the rectitude of their own beliefs.

The printed medium in eighteenth-century America plays a vital role in our knowledge of what the "average colonist" thought and understood about these fundamental matters. And of various forms of print, the newspaper most clearly reflected public attitudes. The high degree of literacy in the colonies, coupled with the wide circulation of newspapers, indicates that the press was of utmost importance in the process of focusing and defining political attitudes.[2]

In speaking of the mid-nineteenth-century newspaper, which differed little in character or nature from its eighteenth-century predecessor, Eric L. McKitrick stated what must be considered a truism: "It is very likely at a time of high feeling that the state of public opinion actually had a great deal more effect on the formation of editorial opinion than the reverse. The great journals of 'influence' in those days did not, as a matter of fact, depend primarily on advertising; they depended on their readers. There is a limit on the extent to which newspapers can 'manufacture' opinion at any time, and there are even greater limits to what they can do to effect reversals of opinion in matters of deep popular convictions. In such cases, 'coercion' and 'manipulation' tend to come, as it were, from the other direction."[3] The validity of this analysis can be seen in the almost total failure of efforts to develop an effective Tory press in the colonies after 1763, except where it received official and financial support from the royal authorities.

The role of the press as a factor in expressing the attitudes of eighteenth-century America toward the basic problems of political thought has recently been challenged by the disturbing view that freedom of the press did not exist in colonial America. Although prior licensing of newspapers had been abandoned as English policy in 1695, it is argued, every printer had hanging over his head the threat of either a seditious libel prosecution under common law or a prosecution for breach of legislative privilege. Thus eighteenth-century America did not "produce or inherit a broad concept of freedom of speech or press," and the words themselves were neither meaningful nor effective.[4] If this is true, the press's influence in forming public opinion is severely diminished and its usefulness as a gauge of public attitudes is highly questionable.

Prosecutions of printers can be documented by court records and legislative journals and, viewed only in this way, a bleak and dismal picture of repression is presented. But a more realistic approach is to look at the newspapers themselves and see what they had to say about the issue. If the press was truly subdued by the threat of official action, that would have been reflected in their statements on their own freedom, or such statements would not have appeared at all.

A few printers were prosecuted in colonial America,[5] but were their cases the rule or the exception? Actually, such prosecutions merely indicated the failure of the eighteenth century to understand freedom fully—not the full absence of any understanding of the subject. If the press of eighteenth-century America sought consistently to define its own freedom, and if those definitions became increasingly precise and widespread, a fair case may be made for the existence of this freedom as a working concept.

Perhaps the basic dilemma is to find and apply an adequate definition. The difficulty of the meaning and nature of freedom is still with us, and we should not be surprised that it plagued our ancestors; rather, we should be encouraged that they were concerned with it. Carl Becker illustrated the difficulty rather well: "The nature of freedom and responsibility," he explained, "is such that they cannot be discussed, still less dealt with, to any good purpose separately. Freedom unrestrained by responsibility becomes mere license; responsibility unchecked by freedom becomes mere abitrary power. The question, then, is . . . how they can be united and reconciled to the best advantage."[6] An eighteenth-century jurist could not have phrased the problem better for his own age.

Newspapers existed in the American colonies long before they engaged in any speculations on their own freedom. Certainly the colonists had an abundance of more mundane concerns in these early years. Still, the absence of such discussion in the first three decades has been puzzling. It is probably explained by the fact that each urban area, until the population expanded adequately, could support but one newspaper, usually an official one that depended on government contracts for economic survival.[7] Not until newspapers began to compete with one another did the question of their freedom arise. Then, as the newcomer sought to break into a monopolistic situation, it found its audience among the opposition faction, and it challenged both the government and the subservience of its longer-established competitor.

Such a situation existed in Boston, for example, where the first competitive newspaper began operation in 1721. James Franklin's *New England Courant* took up the cause of freedom, though in a most guarded way. A letter allegedly coming from "P[ortsmout]h New Hampshire" and signed "Tom. Penshallow" complained: "As for freedom of speech, it is utterly suppressed among us, and I suppose we shall be hanged for our thoughts. . . . It is whispered that we are to have a law prohibiting the reading [of] your Courants . . . because your paper sometimes sets forth the rights and liberties of mankind."[8]

Having labeled himself the enunciator of liberty, James Franklin quickly collided with the Massachusetts authorities. In the summer of 1722 he published a "high affront" to the General Court and was jailed for the balance of the legislative session. Young Benjamin Franklin, the anonymous author of the Silence Dogood letters, responded to the high-handed treatment given his brother by including in one of his letters an extract on freedom of thought from the *London Journal*.[9]

Pretentious behavior continued to be the *Courant's* target: James Franklin attacked religious hypocrisy and cast some aspersions on the recently departed governor in 1723. The House of Representatives immediately ordered that the paper be supervised by the provincial secretary, and Franklin ignored the order.[10] He argued that, if he violated any law, he should be "presented by a grand jury and a fair trial brought on."[11] The *Courant's* editor was then arrested for contempt, and his younger brother became nominal editor. Young Benjamin stated his position succinctly: "It is a vulgar error which some have entertained, and which it concerns every true Englishman to obviate, that there must be no complaint made of the proceeding of the legislative power."[12]

Philadelphia was the next urban center to acquire a competitive newspaper, and the newcomer was Benjamin Franklin, who established the *Pennsylvania Gazette* in 1728. His Boston experience must have left its mark, for he was concerned about the abuse heaped upon printers for publishing materials disliked by those in authority. The business of printing, he editorialized, "has chiefly to do with men's opinions." Consequently, everything a printer did would "probably give offense to some, and perhaps to many." But the printer did not necessarily agree with everything he set in type, nor did he try to limit his columns only to those things of which he personally approved. Franklin's argument, simply enough, was that the printer was a craftsman who should not judge the merits of the ideas he printed, but merely their physical appearance. If the printer turned critic, "the world afterwards would have nothing to read but what happened to be the opinions of printers."[13]

But Franklin begged the question. Who would accept the responsibility shirked by the printer? Andrew Bradford's longer-established *American Weekly Mercury* sought to answer by defining the proper limits of the press. "In all countries where liberty only reigns," wrote an essayist in the *Mercury,* "every man hath a privilege of declaring his sentiments with the utmost freedom; provided he does it with a proper decency and a just regard to the laws." The last phrase imposed the traditional limitations of common law prosecution, but coupled with it was a broader theme: "All governments, under whatever form they are administered, ought to be administered for the good of the society; and when they are otherwise administered, they cease to be government and become usurpation. . . . Even the most despotick have this limitation to their authority." Although, the writer continued, the despotic prince did not have to contend with written constitutional limits, "there is still this tacit condition annexed to his power, that he must act by the unwritten laws of discretion and prudence, and employ it [i.e., power] for the sole interest of the people who give it to him."[14] Suddenly, the definition took on added dimensions, although it was clearly not libertarian when "just regard to the laws" was joined to the concept of limited government.

New York City's first competitive newspaper was John Peter Zenger's *Weekly Journal.* His name immediately arouses memories of the famous trial, which has been analyzed often and well enough by others.[15] Of greater interest is the furor Zenger aroused in the press before and after his trial. He clearly established himself as the opposition printer in the early issues of his paper, and his publication of Gordon and Trenchard's "Cato Letters," two of which dealt with freedom of the press, really began New York's inquiry into freedom.[16]

Letters written anonymously for publication in Zenger's *Journal* soon took up the battle cry, and he published one that dealt with the problem specifically and in absolute terms. "The liberty of the press," it announced, "is a liberty for every man to communicate his sentiments freely to the public, upon political or religious points: it is either this or nothing." Those who feared to expose their pet doctrines to public analysis, the author continued, knew that their ideas stood upon a "very weak foundation," or they were "friends to Popery and arbitrary power."[17]

Zenger continued to publish the "Cato Letters," and one of them finally elicited a response in William Bradford's older *New York Gazette*. "But here is the fallacy, here lies the imposition upon the people," wrote the Bradford essayist, "it would here be insinuated that to punish the licentiousness of the press would be to take away the liberty of the press. . . . Tis the abuse not the use of the press that is criminal and ought to be punished."[18] As the voice of government, this essay expressed traditional attitudes and left undefined the distinction between use and abuse.

Interestingly enough, an answer came from Charleston, South Carolina, where Lewis Timothy's *Gazette* printed a careful analysis of the problem as a lead editorial in his first issue. The idea was simple and powerful: "Neither do I see how any restraint can be put upon the press, in a nation that pretends to liberty, but what is just sufficient to prevent men from writing either blasphemy or treason." The same editorial, slightly amplified by a new introduction, appeared that same week in Andrew Bradford's *American Weekly Mercury* in Philadelphia.[19]

The concentric circles widened, and the discussion of freedom of the press expanded. A series of articles appeared in Philadelphia's *American Weekly Mercury:* the first, while not defining terms, advocated an absolute freedom; the second hit at the real problem.[20] "We must carefully distinguish between liberty and licentiousness," the essayist warned, for "the extremes that separate liberty from license are closer than most men imagine." He began his definitions with negative reasoning: to call into question the King's right to his realm and dominions, or to challenge his private or public life, was "treasonable license." Liberty did not include the subversion of fundamental points of religion and morality. Neither did it include a "license of traducing those gentlemen who are appointed our lawful governors: when they behave themselves well, they ought to be treated with all the respect and gratitude that's due from an obliged people; should they behave themselves ill, their measures are to be remonstrated against in terms of decency and moderation, not of fury or scurrility." Nor should the "sacred veneration" due "the upright dispensers of the law" be altered or destroyed.

The writer concluded with a more positive approach: "by freedom of the press, I mean a liberty, within the bounds of law, for any man to communicate to the public his sentiments on the important points of religion and government; of proposing any laws which he apprehends may be for the good of his country, and of applying for the repeal of such as he judges pernicious. I mean a liberty of detecting the wicked and destructive measures of certain politicians; of dragging villainy out of its obscure lurking holes and exposing it in its full deformity to open day; of attacking wickedness in high places, of disentangling the intricate folds of a wicked and corrupt administration, and pleading freely for a redress of grievances. I mean a liberty of examining the great articles of our faith by the light of scripture and reason."

Although Zenger immediately reprinted this statement in his own *Journal,* it raised more questions than it answered.[21]

Such broadside treatment bothered at least one of Zenger's correspondents. "But how any man can with great satisfaction see that liberty [of the press], the essential liberty of the constitution, enjoyed in so unconfined a manner that some men continue to abuse it . . . with impunity," the writer questioned, "is too deep and intricate for me to understand, unless the person seeing this abuse with so great satisfaction be himself the abuser of it: For I cannot conceive how any man can see a liberty, and an essential liberty of a constitution, abused with impunity, and see that abuse with great satisfaction, too, except himself be the abuser, or some of his friends."[22]

This distinction between use and abuse was of course the key issue. William Bradford's *New York Gazette* sought to clarify it. "I must own," wrote a reader, "that no restraint ought to be put upon the press but what is sufficient to prevent the grossest abuses of it, abuses that dissolute society and sap the very foundation of government . . . but with regard to abuses of a less flagrant nature, I had rather see such permitted than the liberty itself abridged."[23]

The response in Zenger's *Journal* sharpened the issue: "I hope by freely he means without the fear or danger of being punished. When they can so write, it will then be felicitas, and rara felicitas temporum." It is true, the author admitted, "that abuses that dissolve society and sap the foundations of government are not to be sheltered under the umbrage of the liberty of the press: But if those in power will term a trifling song, or anything of so minute a nature, a dissolving of society and sapping of the foundations of government; if they will fix determinate meanings to sentences and even blanks, which the authors have not fixt, and to which other meanings can with equal justice be applied; I would be glad to know wherein this liberty of writing consists?"[24]

This interesting and potentially fruitful dialogue was interrupted by Zenger's arrest for seditious libel in November 1734. Although public attention now shifted to the courtroom, we must pursue the continuing debate in the newspaper columns. Lewis Morris, James Alexander, and Andrew Hamilton all involved themselves in the printer's defense, and they aimed their arguments at winning freedom to criticize for themselves. But in so doing they phrased their arguments in an appealing fashion and, as a result, made them convenient tools for others to use.

The debate began anew when a Barbadian wrote a series of newspaper essays which were reprinted in pamphlet form and given wide distribution. He wanted to destroy the mistaken doctrine that freedom of the press was a "license to write and publish infamous things of their superiors and of all others, at their pleasure, provided they write and publish nothing but what is true." He acknowledged the subject's right to complain to magistrates, parliament, and the King, but he flatly denied the right "of complaining to the neighbors." The press, he declared, is "a two-edged weapon, capable of cutting both ways, and is not therefore to be trusted in the hands of every discontented fool or designing knave. Men of sense and address (who alone deserve public attention) will ever be able to convey proper ideas to the people, in time of danger, without running counter to all order and decency or crying fire and murder thro' the streets if they chance to wake from a frightful dream." Moreover, the right of complaining to the public, even by men of sense and address, was limited to a people in a sovereign state subject to no superior; "this is far from being the case of colonies," he concluded.[25]

This West Indian found his match in a series of essays by James Alexander in the *Pennsylvania Gazette*. Alexander probably felt impelled to respond to the criticism because he had masterminded Zenger's defense, and he probably chose the Philadelphia newspaper because Hamilton, who had been the defense attorney, was being strenuously assaulted by his Pennsylvania enemies because of his role in the trial. The Barbadian's legalistic arguments proved a potent weapon that had to be blunted. The result was what one authority has called the major American contribution to the libertarian theory of the press.[26]

Alexander's arguments began with a statement that republics and limited monarchies derived their strength "from a popular examination into the actions of the magistrates," a privilege which "in all ages has been and always will be abused." Security for the government official, he argued, came not from repression of criticism but from the knowledge that "impartial posterity will not fail to render him justice." Freedom of speech and press would be abused—"these are the excrescences of liberty"—and "they ought to be suppressed." But, he asked, "to whom dare we commit the care of doing it?" To give this to a magistrate would place too much power in his hands—"under pretense of pruning off the exuberant branches, he frequently destroys the tree."

Tracing the doctrine of seditious libel from Augustus Caesar to the days of the Stuarts, Alexander dwelled on the famous case of Algernon Sydney and concluded that a grave danger "attends a law for punishing words." There was little security for men when "a judge by remote inferences and distant innuendos may construe the most innocent expressions into capital crimes." Rather suffer an inconveniency, he warned, "when it cannot be removed without introducing a worse."

Alexander concluded on the theme that it was every man's duty to "expose the evil designs or weak management of a magistrate. . . . To suppress inquiries into the administration is a good policy in an arbitrary government. But a free constitution and freedom of speech have a reciprocal dependence on each other; that they cannot subsist without consisting together."[27]

The debate, once narrowly focused between Governor Cosby and his opponents in New York, had now spread to become something far more important. New ideas had been broached which could not be suppressed, and they reappeared in the most unusual places and contexts. Moreover, each time they were applied, they were further refined.

One illustration of this was the proposal by Andrew Bradford and John Webbe to publish a magazine in Philadelphia. In the initial announcement, Webbe assured his prospective subscribers that the magazine would adhere to freedom of the press. Its pages would be open to all contenders but "would carefully avoid contributing to the licentiousness of the press." By this he meant "defamatory libeling, as it comprehends the ideas of falsehood and scandal combined together." After citing Hamilton's arguments in Zenger's defense, Webbe proceeded to scriptural evidence. "We are there commanded to pay obedience to governors, yet not to all generally, but only to those who use their authority for the punishment of evildoers and for the praise of them that do well. . . . Where the end of government is perverted, it is criminal in any man to acquiesce under it." He qualified his libertarianism with a plea for practicality; should a people "be reduced to the unhappy necessity of making such public remonstrances . . . [it was hoped] that the management of them might always be reserved for men of skill and address. It is not for every puny arm to attempt to wield the club of Hercules."[28]

Freedom as a whole served as the topic for an extended essay by Jeremiah Gridley in the *American Magazine and Historical Chronicle*, published in Boston by Rogers and Fowle. In dealing with the specific problem of freedom of thought, which encompassed the press as a means of expression, Gridley asserted that he had the right in a state of nature to read Homer, or Virgil, or Horace. Upon entering a political society intended "to support my life and property and civil interests," he retained that liberty. "For from what source can such a society derive a right to hinder my studies, recreations, or amusements, which do not affect the ends of society?" While the last clause limited his concept of freedom, Gridley later strengthened it with a nautical analogy. After declaring that man by entering society actually acquired a liberty of speaking his sentiments openly on anything affecting the good of the whole, he continued: "Wherever therefore he perceives a rock upon which there is a probability that the vessel may split, or if he sees a shoal or sand that may swallow it up, or if he foresees a storm likely to arise, his interest is too deeply concerned not to give notice of the danger. And the right he has to life and property gives him a right to speak his sentiments. If the pilot of the ship refuses to hear, or if the captain will take no notice, yet 'tis certain they acquire no right to punish the well-meant information, nor to stop the mouth of him who thinks he decries danger to the whole ship's crew."[29]

The Boston *Independent Advertiser* sharpened the awareness of freedom with a conscious effort to define terms. "Perhaps no words have been more misunderstood or perverted," stated an essayist, "than the words loyalty and sedition. The former I take to signify a firm and inviolable attachment to a legal constitution, the latter, all tendencies, machinations, and attempts to overset a legal constitution." It was a great mistake, he continued, "to imagine that the object of loyalty is the authority and interest of one individual man, however dignified by the applause or enriched by the success of popular actions. . . . The true object of loyalty is a good legal constitution, which as it condemns every instance of oppression and lawless power, derives a certain remedy to the sufferer by allowing him to remonstrate his grievances and pointing out methods of relief when the gentler arts of persuasion have lost their efficacy."[30]

This author had certainly reached for a significant idea. By clarifying the term to which loyalty and sedition must necessarily refer, he weakened the case for seditious libel. When the subject is loyal to an inanimate object, a document, or a set of generally accepted rules, rather than a personality, we have a modern democratic state. Although no other newspaper reprinted this particular essay, none sought to rebut it. Indeed, the same idea would reappear in different dress before 1763.

Still another variation on this theme was supplied by James Parker in the *New York Gazette*. "How can any branch of our liberties be said to be safe," he argued, "if we have not the liberty of complaining of any attempt to take it away? Though liberty be a joint stock, in respect to the nation, yet every individual has his property therein; and the security he has for't is his right of appealing to the public if it's invaded or taken away. . . . False and foolish complaints are often brought, but then they are brought to no purpose, or, at least, the bringing them answer no ill purpose. On the contrary, the contempt with which they are treated manifest the candor and impartiality of the public; and this ought not therefore to be set up as an argument for suppressing that tribunal"—meaning the press.[31]

This theme soon spread. The *New York Mercury* published an item which the *Pennsylvania Gazette* immediately picked up. "The licentiousness of the press is, in the eyes of some people, an extraordinary grievance, and oblique threats are thrown out that as it deserves, so it will meet with a restriction. Be that day far from us! . . . But the press may be abused. What is there then that may not? The Bible may be abused, the laws may be abused, the constitution may be abused, yet we have a birthright in them all, and we should be miserable if they were taken from us."[32]

A more sophisticated and thorough analysis appeared shortly thereafter in the "Watch Tower #10," published in the *New York Mercury* and reprinted in the *Virginia Gazette*. "The most interesting objects of knowledge to men in society are religion, either natural or revealed, and government. To the study of which the downright priest and despotic ruler generally claim an exclusive right. It is, however, the proper business of an intelligent being to investigate those relations of his existence which either bestow on him some privileges or subject him to certain duties. . . . If no law can be binding upon the subject without his consent, he has surely a right to divulge his sentiments, either relating to the conduct of the person intrusted with the execution of the laws; or of those, who, intrusted with certain powers for the public good, convert them to private and sinister uses; such persons being all creatures of that constitution or body of laws to the making of which his assent was absolutely necessary."

"It is true," continued the "Watch Tower," that "by a variety of adjudged cases, in our law books, the publication of any writing which charges a person in office with the commission of a crime or exposes him to popular odium and reflection is not the less libelous for being true. Which piece of law is founded upon this reason, that tho a libel be true, yet it may tend to stir up sedition or cause a breach of the peace; and therefore the law relating to libels may sometimes be wholesome. But as every general rule admits of some exceptions, so in particular cases a state may be ruined by the persons to whom the management is committed, for want of timely notice to those whose interest, were they apprized of the danger, would urge them to the utmost exertion of their abilities in its support. And if a people can be presumed to have a right in any instance to oppose the undue measures of an arbitrary ruler when they strike at the very vitals of the constitution, they are certainly justifiable in opposing them not only with the pen but even with the sword. And then, what becomes of the reason upon which the above law, relating to libels, is founded?" Libel charges in lesser matters could easily be avoided because an official could be calumniated by "a writing that inveighs against a particular order of men and does not descend to individuals of that order." Such a writing "is no libel."[33]

Once again an essayist had hinted at the way to destroy the weapon of seditious libel. The theme enunciated earlier in the Boston *Independent Advertiser* had been repeated seven years later. If officeholders are the creatures of the constitution, and if men's loyalties are to that instrument rather than to the person exercising the office, seditious libel as a repressive device loses its value. Although the "Watch Tower" essayist did not pursue this as closely as the earlier article had, in a sense he went even further by arguing that the people have a right to oppose arbitrary rulers by sword as well as pen.

The sharpening of definitions continued. An article by "W.K." in the *Boston Gazette* took an even more absolute view and incorporated freedom of speech and thought as well. "Without freedom of thought, there can be no such thing as wisdom; and no such thing as public liberty, without freedom of speech: Which is the right of every man as far as by it he does not hurt and control the right of another; and this is the only check which it ought to suffer, the only bounds which it ought to know. . . . That men ought to speak well of their governors is true, while their governors deserve to be well spoken of, but to do public mischief, without hearing of it, is only the prerogative and felicity of tyranny."[34]

The theme of freedom was expanding rapidly. A piece for the *Connecticut Gazette,* supposedly written by James Parker, admitted that "a darling so carefully guarded and powerfully supported" might occasionally grow "wanton and luxurious" and abuse its power. But the press must be permitted to go beyond the bounds normally prescribed by reason in order that its just freedom be preserved inviolate. To lay the least restraint upon it, no matter how justified, would open the way for improper and unreasonable restrictions and would cause it to lose its "salutary influence." Further, an overextension of liberty for the press could be justified "because it carries [within itself] the means of restraining, or reducing itself to its proper boundaries." By this the essayist meant that "the freedom of animadversion, even upon the press itself, being included in the liberty thereof, its extravagances must soon be suppressed, and it must be reduced to the limits prescribed by reason." The true definition of freedom, the author emphasized, was that "none can complain that the same liberty was not allowed impartially to every one. Whoever was displeased at any thing that has been published might have made his objections as public as the cause of them."[35]

This, indeed, was true freedom of the press. The article attributed to Parker was not alone in its view that the government had no power to restrain or punish printing. The *Boston Gazette* elaborated on it in 1756 and in 1758. "'Tis true, where there is liberty there may be licentiousness. But this is as true of every other liberty as that of the tongue or pen. And if 'tis reasonable our tongues or pens should be subjected to the control of appointed inspectors, lest they should be misused, 'tis reasonable that our liberty, in all other instances, should be restrained in like manner; that is, we ought to be enslaved to prevent our making an ill-use of our freedom."[36] Two years later the same paper returned to the argument: "Every Briton . . . has therefore a right to think for himself on all public affairs, and if he pleases to think aloud;—This privilege like all others should be used with discretion, but not to have it at all, or never to improve it, is the same thing. . . . Let both sides then speak freely, and by the collision the sparks of truth may leap out."[37]

In 1762 Weyman's *New York Gazette* prophetically summed up the newspapers' views of their own freedom and utility. "It is to this bringing grievances before the tribunal of the public that we owe every good law that has been passed within our memory; and though it may be true that there are many grievances still unredressed, against which long complaints have been often made, yet this is no just objection. For tho' they are not yet redressed, they may and will be in time. . . . But there is another very good effect which may be looked upon as certain, though we can afford no proof of it; it is this, that many more grievances we should have had if this remedy was not always in our power; and many more grievances we certainly shall have if ever it is taken from us; which under the English constitution we have no reason to fear; because that constitution can fear nothing from it."[38]

"The persistent image of colonial America," writes Leonard Levy, "as a society in which freedom of expression was cherished is an hallucination of sentiment that ignores history."[39] He is correct, but only in part. It was a society engaged in learning the value of such freedom and defining, albeit haltingly at times, its meaning. By the 1760's, however, it had developed a viable definition, one which was circulated widely enough for one to conclude that it had attained public acceptance. By defining the object of loyalty more precisely, the press had blunted the weapon of seditious libel; by identifying itself with the forces of self-government, the press had reduced the need for legislative repression; by urging that its columns be open to all, the press had safely channeled criticism. The way now was open for the newspaper, despite occasional efforts to repress its exuberance, to become a basic political force in the imperial crisis of the 1760's and 1770's. To be certain, the hysteria of the revolution would jeopardize this definition of freedom, but its speedy and easy recovery is more worthy of note than the aberration.

II

The State of Nature
and the Origin
of Government

BASIC to an understanding of the theory of government is man's view of what existed before the creation of society. Upon this foundation rest his ideas as to why government was established and as to what, consequently, its nature, purpose, and function should be. In eighteenth-century America two main ideas, two basic approaches, contended with each other. Thomas Hobbes's views reflected the ideas of the English Civil War era, while John Locke's concepts codified English thought at the time of the Glorious Revolution a generation later.

Hobbes offered a pessimistic view of man's condition in the state of nature, which he considered to have a philosophical rather than an historical existence. This distinction allowed him to argue that the social contract was an arrangement between subject and subject rather than subject and ruler. Such reasoning readily led to a concept of the state in which the subject is powerless and can exert no control over his destiny. In simple terms, Hobbes advocated unlimited obedience to the sovereign.

Locke, on the other hand, took a more optimistic view of

man in a state of nature which to him had been a real, not imaginary, period of existence. At that time man lived under rules and regulations, not jungle-like conditions, and that framework was the law of nature. This seemingly idyllic condition was abandoned for society and government, which he viewed as two separate entities, because each person was unable to avail himself of the full protection of natural law for his person and property. Society and government thus came into being as supplements to rather than replacements for natural law or right reason, and therefore they must abide by it. When they depart from natural law, they collapse. The Lockean interpretation of the state of nature includes of necessity the right of revolution whenever government fails to fulfill the function for which it was created—an unsettling thought which Thomas Hobbes would have rejected.

With both ideas in circulation in eighteenth-century America, it is somewhat surprising at first glance that few adhered to the more pessimistic Hobbes thesis. But an examination of the Americans' experience leads one quickly to the conclusion that Locke's appeal was bound to be greater. The Americans had entered a new world with no guidelines but those of their own past experience. They set up governments in the wilderness, but they certainly believed they established them on "right reason." There was little in what they were doing to suggest that they were living through the Hobbesian jungle. Moreover, in the garrison century from 1603 to 1689 they had been forced to adjust and modify government according to their immediate local needs, without waiting for directions from the Crown and often in contradiction to Crown policy.[1] Thus the ideas expressed by Locke were indeed meaningful; they were a rationalization of the Americans' own experience.

Few writers in eighteenth-century America gave more than cursory attention to the theories of Hobbes. His view of the state of nature was described by the redoubtable Cotton Mather as this "detestable Hobbianism" according to which "men are as the fishes of the sea, to one another; where the greater still devour the lesser." Although Mather rejected his ideas outright, Hobbes did have a few advocates. The Reverend Samuel Cheever warned that government was God's ordinance "that men might not live as beasts. . . . Licentious nature doth not love to be controlled, and would have no lord over it; but sound reason will tell every man that there is no living where every man may do what he will without control."[2] When Archibald Cummings delivered the funeral sermon for Lieutenant Governor Patrick Gordon of Pennsylvania, he warned the quarrelsome inhabitants of the colony that without government men would turn "into beasts of prey" because they would be freed of all legal restraints. This denied Locke's basic point that the law of nature antedated government's establishment. Later, in 1755, the Reverend Moses Dickinson returned to the same theme when he declared that men were mutually dependent upon one another, and that without the restraints of civil society "we should be in a state of confusion; like an herd of wild beasts; the strongest, and most mischievous, would domineer over and oppress others. There would be no peace, to him that should go out, or to him that should come in; our lives, and properties . . . would . . . depend upon the ungoverned lusts of the sons of fraud and violence. . . . To suppose (as some have done) that mankind were ever in such a mere state of nature as to have no laws, no regulations, no sort of government, is to suppose a contradiction; for such a wild and savage state could not with any propriety be called a state of nature; for it would be a very unnatural state."[3]

These were not the views of the majority of those Americans who expressed themselves in print. The Lockean concepts dominated men's imaginations from the beginning and soon became a crescendo overwhelming the ideas of Cheever, Cummings, and Dickinson. One cannot even claim that Hobbes's theory was advocated by any particular group or class in American society because, even though a few Congregationalist clergymen embraced Hobbesian concepts, most spokesmen for this denomination stood at the very forefront of Lockean ideas, not only advocating them but refining and making them more precisely applicable to the American scene.

Perhaps the first Congregational minister to declaim the ideas of John Locke was Thomas Maule. "In the beginning," he wrote in 1712, "when men grew numerous they contracted themselves into societies, for preservation of concord and good discipline, and began to think on foundations to set their structures upon. . . . First, the civil society united that they might live safely and enjoy their liberties without opposition."[4] His concern was with the separation of civil and ecclesiastical societies, but his use of the word "preservation" implies acceptance of the Lockean approach. When men multiplied to the point that conflict became inevitable and prior existing liberties were challenged, society came into being to facilitate man's enjoyment of what he already possessed.

This same theme was developed by the Reverend John Wise in greater detail five years later. Man in a state of "natural being," he observed in his famous *Vindication,* was a "freeborn subject under the crown of heaven, and owing homage to none but God himself." Man's "prime immunity" was that "he is most properly the subject of the law of nature. . . . Reason is cognate with his nature, wherein by a law immutable, stamped upon his frame, God has provided a rule for men in all their actions . . . which is nothing but the dictate of right reason founded in the soul of man. . . . That which is to be drawn from man's reason . . . when unperverted, may be said to be the law of nature. . . . When we acknowledge the law of nature to be the dictate of right reason, we must mean that the understanding of man is endowed with such a power as to be able from the contemplation of humane condition to discover a necessity of living agreeably with this law." These principles of natural law, Wise continued, could be discovered "by a narrow watch, and accurate contemplation of our natural condition, and propensions."

For John Wise, natural law contained three principles: self-love and self-preservation, sociable disposition, and an affection to mankind in general. While self-love and self-preservation were basic, man was often incapable of securing his safety and maintenance alone, and thus the need for the second principle —sociability. "Every man as far as in him lies, do maintain a sociableness with others, agreeable with the main end and disposition of humane nature in general." The third principle emerged from the fact that man was not so wedded to self-interest that he was blinded to the advantages of the common good, and it is this which encouraged him to enter society.[5]

Maule and Wise were theologically oriented commentators. A secular interpretation of the same problem came from John Webbe, who wrote a series of newspaper essays in 1736 under the pseudonym "Z." He began with the statement that men were born equal and subject to no superior. Thus when men relinquished liberty, they did so for "a more valuable consideration, as protection from injuries, security of property, mutual defense, etc."

To Webbe, Hobbes's idea that people confer all of their power permanently upon a ruler was merely a "specious pretext." If the state of nature "is a state of war, which implies a natural equality, I presume I have as much right to repel wrongs as another has to impose them. Yet, say the Hobbists, it is our interest to submit to be governed by the will of one man. I would feign ask . . . how they [rulers] came by such a social affection? Whence, all this tenderness for their fellow creatures? It cannot be hypocrisy, as they have openly declared themselves to be villains in grain. It must therefore proceed from a natural irresistible impulse."[6]

Still another secular explanation of Lockean theory appeared in the speech of Chief Justice Samuel Chew to the Newcastle County grand jury in 1741. Life and liberty, he stated, "were common to all men," and each had a natural title to their full enjoyment and a right to preserve and defend them. "If, indeed, all men, from the beginning, had acted up to the genuine law of nature, and had done what was perfectly right, all other provisions or laws would have been useless." But rapaciousness and corruption entered the world, and "it is more than probable that men in a state of nature . . . must have suffered much." Their desire for happiness and the instinct of self-preservation led them into compacts. The difference, Chew continued, between men in a state of nature and in political societies was the absence in the former of a common judge, with every man having the right to judge and punish for himself. Such judgments were based on "the law of reason, or . . . a rule for the doing what is fit and proper for rational creatures to do as they are capable of discovering by the right use of the natural faculties, unassisted by supernatural revelation."[7]

The general enthusiasm for Lockean theory had to overcome certain criticisms of technical aspects of the state of nature. One of the serious ones was the lack of historical evidence of such a state. Hobbes had avoided this problem by posing his state of nature as a philosophical concept, but Locke had argued that it had actually existed in the beginning of all things. Jared Eliot, in his Hartford election sermon of 1738, answered those who criticized on this point. The fact that no records of such a state existed proved nothing, said Eliot, since government itself antedated record-keeping.[8]

A further criticism of Locke was the anomaly of the status of children. It was all well and good to talk of man's liberty either in the state of nature or society, but who would insist upon the same liberty for a young child? These critics argued that if man was born into a state of nature, and if that situation was governed by natural law or right reason, and if man must use his rational faculties to control his situation, how then did one explain the subservient position of the child to his parent and the child's utter inability to use right reason?

This contrast between the theoretical equality of men and the practical problem of parental rule was tackled by Elisha Williams in 1744. Children were "not born in this full state of equality, yet they are born to it," he announced. Parental jurisdiction was temporary until reason matured in the child. "When he comes to such a state of reason as made the father free, the same must make the son free too." Freedom was grounded on reason, and therefore it "is not a liberty for everyone to do what he pleases . . . but it consists in a freedom from any superior power on earth . . . and having only the law of nature (or in other words, of its maker) for his rule."

Williams also expounded on the role of property in the state of nature. The earth was granted by God in common to all men, and since each man's principal property was his own person, the labor of his body is his own. When he "removes anything out of the state that nature has provided and left it in, he has mixed his labor with it and joined something to it that is his own, and thereby makes it his property." If each person had a right to his person, he had a right to the property created by his bodily efforts, and concomitantly the right to punish all insults to either. This led to the question of providing protection, and Williams then quoted Locke on the three factors lacking in the state of nature to render the individual and his property safe: an established law to distinguish right from wrong, an indifferent judge, and a power to execute sentence against wrongdoers. Reason, Williams believed, taught men to remedy these defects by uniting in society.[9]

A panegyric in the Boston *Independent Advertiser* in 1749 reaffirmed this concept of the state of nature. "The perfection of liberty, therefore, in a state of nature, is for every man to be free from any external force and to perform such actions as in his own mind and conscience he judges to be rightest. . . . This is liberty in a state of nature; which as no man ought to be abridged of, so no man has a right to give up, or even to part with any portion of it, but in order to secure the rest and place it upon a more solid foundation. . . . And had mankind continued in that innocent and happy state . . . it is probable that this liberty would have been enjoyed in such perfection as to have rendered the embodying into civil society and the security of human laws altogether needless."[10]

William Livingston, in one issue of his *Independent Reflector,* dwelt on the idea of the state of nature. "Men of true principles would rather return to a state of primitive freedom," he declared, "in which every man has a right to be his own carver, than be the slaves of the greatest monarch or even suffer under the most unlimited democracy in the universe. It is true that society is the most eligible state in which man can exist; nor can it also be denied that government is absolutely necessary for the happiness of society. But still, it will appear . . . to be the height of madness to purchase the advantages of society by giving up all our title to liberty. . . . Had man been wise from his creation, he would always have been free. We might have enjoyed the gifts of liberal nature unmolested, unrestrained."[11]

Livingston's statement incorporated the Lockean assumption that the state of nature involved absolute equality. A sharp criticism appeared in 1753 in the *New York Mercury:* Livingston "must appear very absurd, and very far from acting rationally himself, when he would pawn upon his readers an old contract of very great importance to them, of which he produces no record, nor any footsteps, but from his own notions of absurdity, and suppositions that mankind in a state of nature must needs have acted rationally."

The same critic declared that mankind seemed to have been under some government from the very beginning of his existence, and that "no man was ever so independent as that he might do whatever was right in his own eyes. If Adam and Cain, the first of mankind, were accountable for their actions, when could any others claim the liberty of Mr. Reflector's state of nature and his original native power in man?" Power emanated from God, and it was His will, without compacts, that was imposed on men from the beginning.[12]

But such carping was swept aside by a flurry of support for the Lockean theory in the 1750's and early 1760's. "Rusticus" in Boston discussed the qualities of the state of nature by quoting Locke. "Plebeian" in the *Pennsylvania Journal,* followed by the "Watchman" in the same paper, reiterated similar interpretations. The Reverend Abraham Williams summed up the argument most effectively in his 1762 election sermon in Boston. Indeed, one can almost claim unanimity of viewpoint when he envisions a Congregational minister delivering an election sermon to the Massachusetts General Court and completely paraphrasing John Locke![13]

Although Americans in the eighteenth century seemed to agree upon their definition of the state of nature, their concept of the origin of government and its nature and purpose was much more controversial. They could and did acquiesce in the myth of man's original purity and his early apostasy, but the question of government itself hit close to home, and the colonists' reactions to it depended more immediately on their attitude toward local, everyday problems.

Perhaps the earliest discussion of the origin of government was in the Reverend Samuel Willard's 1694 election sermon. He chose for his topic "The Character of a Good Ruler." He acknowledged the controversy over the origin of government—whether it was a law of nature invoked as mankind increased

in number, or a positive right introduced upon man's apostasy
—and concluded that God, even in a state of nature, had
ordained orders of superiority and inferiority, and since man's
unhappy fall from grace, "necessity requires and the political
happiness of a people is concerned in the establishment of civil
government."

To Willard the purpose of government was "to prevent and
cure the disorders that are apt to break forth among the societies of men; and to promote the civil peace and prosperity of
such a people, as well as to suppress impiety and to nourish
religion." Civil rulers, he continued, "are God's Viceregents
here upon earth; hence they are sometimes honored with the
title of Gods. . . . Government is God's ordinance; and those
that are vested with it, however mediately introduced into it,
have their rightful authority from Him." Willard's absolutist
notion of government was later weakened when he admitted
that "people are not made for rulers, but rulers for a people.
It is indeed an honor which God puts upon some above others
. . . but it is for the people's sake. . . . And, however they are
seated in authority by men, yet God, who rules over all, hath
put them in only Durante Bene Placito. . . . They are stewards,
and whensoever God pleaseth, He will call for a reckoning and
put them out." Civil authority was not given to certain persons
or families by natural right, nor did God determine the form
of government. Sometimes He pointed to persons or families,
sometimes He "judicially delivers a people up to the will of
their enemies," and sometimes He permitted a voluntary arrangement by the free consent of the people. But regardless of
the method, His hand was always evident.[14]

The ultimate consequence of this God-oriented political
philosophy was simply expressed by the Reverend Ebenezer
Pemberton in 1710: "Rebellion and disobedience against God's
Viceregents in the lawful execution of their office is rebellion
against God himself."[15] But this left several important questions unanswered. How did one determine whom God had

chosen? How did one know whether the ruler was following God's dictates or his own? What marked off the bounds of "lawful execution"? If the answer to these questions was the ruler himself, then the circle was complete, and so was the absolutism. If the answer was the clergy, the circle had simply been enlarged slightly, and the concept had progressed from autocracy to theocracy.

As long as the Congregational clergy of New England remained the most vocal exponents of political thought, the idea that government was God's blessing to mankind remained dominant. The first significant dissent came from Thomas Maule in 1712, who said that when men "grew numerous they contracted themselves into societies. . . . First, the civil society united, that they might live safely and enjoy their liberty without opposition, and [then] they were united into churches to live religiously." But the more traditional theme was restated by John Woodward's Hartford election sermon in the same year. Civil rulers, he announced, were "ministers of the great God, to whom obedience is undoubtedly due." He acknowledged that all forms of government were not divinely ordained, but power itself was. This was seconded by the Boston election sermon of Samuel Cheever that same year.[16]

The first major break in the united approach of the Congregational ministers came with the Hartford election sermon of the Reverend Joseph Moss in 1715. "All just government, whether it be monarchy or popular, or a mixture of both, or of any differing form, is originally founded in either compact or conquest." If created by compact, the authority of government was limited. "None can make a just claim to any natural original right to rule over others . . . so mankind never did nor will submit themselves voluntarily to the government of others their fellow-men, but upon some agreement of what rules the ruler or rulers should observe."[17] For the first time, new answers had been offered to some of the basic questions.

Moss' position was non-absolutist, and another theologian

—the Reverend John Wise in 1717—adopted a similar stance. "The formal reason of government is the will of a community, yielded up and surrendered to some other subject." The method used to accomplish this came straight from Locke: first, men covenanted with one another to join in society; next, a government was established by the majority; and, finally, a new covenant was created between the society and the rulers. Wise's definition of a civil government was simply: "a compound moral person, whose will (united by those covenants before passed) is the will of all; to the end it may use and apply the strength and riches of private persons towards maintaining the common peace, security, and well-being of all."[18]

Yet there were not many in the early eighteenth century who adopted such advanced thought. The ideas of Wise and Moss seem to be departures from the generally accepted tendency to view government in an absolutist sense. That view was not limited to theologians, for an admiralty judge, in sentencing two culprits for contempt of the Crown, declared in 1721: "If we consult the law of God, that will tell us that the powers which be are ordained of God: If we will hear the voice of Reason, that will convince us that . . . our own preservation requires us to pay a dutiful obedience to the prince.

> Curse not the king,
>   no not in thy thoughts;
> For the birds of the air
>   will reveal the secret,
> And that which hath wings
>   will utter the voice."[19]

But this authoritarianism contained within itself the seeds of self-destruction. Or, to put it another way, there was inherent in these statements a way out of the dilemma. If government was ordained by God, and if the powers of government were given to certain individuals by God, and if the purpose of these arrangements was the protection and happiness of men, some method must be available to remedy a ruler's perversion of God's intent. One of the first to explore this path was the Congregationalist minister William Burnham in 1722: "Civil rulers are to be obeyed in that which is lawful, otherwise we must obey God rather than man."[20]

Burnham's theme was picked up in a letter in the *New England Courant* in 1722: "Civil government (when . . . regulated by the Divine Standard) is the strength, glory, and safety of nations and commonwealths. . . . The great design of God in the institution of government among men, was . . . the weal and happiness of those who are governed. . . . The power of civil rulers is derivative and limited, and therefore they must not arrogate to themselves an absolute uncontrollable empire, which appertains to God alone. . . . When men in high places assume despotic power . . . they rebel against heaven. . . . The power of civil rulers is but a ministry under God, derived from Him and designed by Him for the good of man. . . . Princes and judges of the earth are gods by office, and they act like such when justice and truth are the steady basis of their thrones. . . . When they act contrary hereto, there belongs another name to them, too horrible to be mentioned . . . and consequently [they] expose themselves to divine resentments and the heavy curses of their people."[21]

Now there were potentially effective limits prescribed for government. If "men in high places" rebelled against God, they lost His protection. All that was lacking was the definition of what constituted their rebellion. The *Courant* letter was still vague on this point: the revolt occurred when the rulers assumed "despotic power," when they abandoned "justice and truth." Once those terms could be given more precision, the next logical step would be the right of the ruled to determine the existence of rebellion by their rulers.

Although no one had yet had the temerity to define the limits of the ruler's power, a more secular, more non-absolutist approach which would eventually demand such a definition was beginning to permeate colonial thought. Sir William Keith, speaking to the corporation of Newcastle in 1724, announced: "Government of any society is only the voluntary establishment of an artificial but just force, upon every individual person, to discharge such obligations as he has received from the public or his neighbor, with justice and gratitude."[22] There was no longer even a hint of the role of God in government.

Five years later the *Pennsylvania Gazette* elaborated on this theme. "The original of all power is in the people"; government was created as "a bulwark against the depredations of an open enemy, or the designing craft of a hypocrite"; if men observed the law of nature, government would be unnecessary, but by experience it was known that men differed. All could not legislate, and therefore trust was reposed in a few who had the time and inclination to do so efficaciously. "Hence government arises with all its beauties when that trust is discharged with honor; but as power is of an increasing nature thro' the weakness and imperfections of human kind, what was designed to support us in our rightful liberties sometimes springs up into unlimited prerogative." Absolute government, the *Gazette* concluded, "implies a renouncing [of] their reasoning." This new attitude toward government was reinforced by "Philo-Patriae" in John Peter Zenger's newspaper: "Civil government was first introduced to guard the safety of mankind . . . and every man in his wits will confess, that 'tis a sin of a very heinous kind to oppose a lawful ruler, whilst acting within the limits of his authority."[23]

What was perhaps most significant about such essays was their acceptance of the fact that absolutism was wrong, that government was a trust, and that the ruler operated within limits prescribed to his authority. Even the clergy were beginning to imbibe this new wine, and they began viewing the divine role more as a limiting factor than as one transferring all authority directly from God to the ruler. According to Jeremiah Wise in 1729, God gave rulers their powers, but He did it mediately not immediately, and "according to the divers constitutions of kingdoms and states." Moreover, as He granted power, He limited it "by His word and providence." Governors operated under "fixed rules, even the rules of God's word, and humane laws agreeable thereto." The Reverend Nathaniel Chauncey's 1734 election sermon went so far as to describe the origin of government without once mentioning God. Civil government, he stated, was man's invention to replace God's rule after the apostasy. It was created when "mankind have generally consented, to leave that state of natural freedom to judge for themselves, and so resign it into the hands of a public ruler."[24]

This is not to suggest that all Boston clergymen shared Chauncey's opinion. John Barnard firmly declared in the same year that government arose from God, "who is the God of order and not of confusion." The existence of government was not left to man's option, it was not "a matter of liberty and freedom." Rather, it "comes to us with a thus saith the Lord." Since divine power formed and fitted man for society, it was obvious that omnipotent reason had also fitted society to man's needs. Government then simply became man's subjection to laws concerning his conduct with his Maker and his fellow creatures. Barnard went so far as to suggest that government was necessary even in Eden, because man was a fallible creature needing rules to guide his actions, although the form of government in a state of innocence was far different from that necessary in a state of apostasy.

Barnard did not, however, connect the divine necessity of government with any divine preference as to its form. He openly declared that "it remains with any civil society to alter and change the form of their government when they see just reason for it and all parties are consenting." He went even further by denying the "Adamitical" or patriarchal concept of the divine right of rulers, doing so in a statement that a Thomas Paine might have found acceptable: "After all is said, the right to rule takes its rise from the consent and agreement, that is the choice and election, of the community, state, or kingdom."[25]

The earlier rigidity of the theologians appeared to be softening. Ideas which had been dominant in the seventeenth century, and which in their strength had spilled over into the eighteenth, were now being significantly modified. Jared Eliot's 1738 election sermon in Hartford suggested the growing secularism that had invaded the political thought of the clergy. "Civil government is set up by force, fraud, or by compact," he declared. It is created by the necessity of resolving hostilities among people. "Whether this union be from a principle of fear or love of society, or from both, has been a matter of dispute. But that some kind of government is for the good of mankind is beyond all dispute."[26]

When Chief Justice Samuel Chew addressed the Newcastle County grand jury in 1741, there was little evidence of theology in his description of government. "The natural desire then of happiness and that principle of self-preservation, common to all men, must first have inspired them, for their common protection and safety, with notions of compacts, of laws, and of governments, as absolutely necessary, and without which it was impossible for them to be happy in any degree." The Governor of Virginia, addressing the House of Burgesses, spoke in a similar vein: "The expectation of faring better under such civil combinations than when living separately is the origin of all communities, the great purpose for which government was created." And Chief Justice Chew, a year later, reiterated his position: "The end of all civil government being happiness, that happiness consists in the security and protection of the lives, liberties, and properties of the people who form or constitute the community."[27]

These highly secular approaches to the origin and purpose of government effectively eliminated concepts of divine right and ensconced Lockean theory firmly in the American mind. Elisha Williams proclaimed in 1744: "The fountain and original of all civil power is from the people, and is certainly instituted for their sakes; or in other words . . . the great end of civil government is the preservation of their persons, their liberties and estates, or their property." It was by this means that men filled the voids that existed in the state of nature—the lack of established law, an indifferent judge, and a power to carry out sentence against wrongdoers. "It is they who thus unite together, viz., the people, who make and alone have a right to make the laws that are to take place among them; which comes to the same thing, appoint those who shall make them, and who shall see them executed."[28]

There were still echoes of the older theological approach abroad in the land. The Reverend James Allen delivered an election sermon in 1744 and challenged the secular interpretation of government's origin. "An ungoverned society of men would be no better than a herd of savage beasts, worrying and devouring one another. . . . To prevent this confusion, God has instituted civil government to be a guard upon our persons and lives." But Allen admitted certain limits. The fact that government was "an institution of Christ" did not mean that "any particular form of it is so," for the Apostle expressly stated that the form "is an human ordinance." He also admitted the absurdity of stating that kings and governors "are sent down immediately from Heaven, with their commissions in their hands." The power of rulers, Allen acknowledged, flowed from the constitutions they were under, and they were limited by those constitutions to doing that "which is just and right to all under that constitution."

Allen thus accepted the divine origin of government but not of governors. He went further by agreeing that rulers who exercised illegal authority need not be obeyed. When a ruler extended his authority beyond its proper limits, man had a "duty to disobey. . . . God must be obeyed rather than man." Unfortunately, Allen failed to provide the necessary guidelines for determining the bounds of lawful authority, and he also neglected to spell out the recourses available to the subject in the event a ruler acted illegally.[29]

Allen's sermon provided a concession by the clergy to the growing tide of secularism. He could not admit that God played no role whatsoever in the establishment of so basic an institution as government, but he had agreed that the forms, powers, and authorities of government were all human devices. In a 1746 election sermon, Samuel Hall repeated much of Allen's position. "And among the various forms," Hall declared, "one is calculated for a people under such and such circumstances; another for people under different circumstances." This meant that monarchies, aristocracies, and even democracies could be justified, although Hall preferred tyranny to democracy because the only danger came from "the enormities of a few" rather than a situation in which "everyone is a tyrant."[30]

An essay by "Layman" in 1747 challenged these clerical concessions to secularism. Written as a gloss on the first seven verses of the thirteenth chapter of St. Paul to the Romans, the argument was rather obvious. "All temporal government that is established in any country is of God, tho' it's done and acted by man, yet it's by God's permission and appointment." As a consequence, man had no right to dispute how the "supreme magistrate" came by his power, or whether it was lawful. "Whoever has got the government in their hands, it immediately becomes our duty to become subject." The only limitation, and a weak one at that, was that men should not act "contrary to our duty to God."[31]

An anonymous correspondent quickly responded in the same journal. Government was ordained and instituted by God, the essayist admitted, but He limited it "to be exercised according to the laws of nature." Governors were designed by God to act for the "safety, welfare, and prosperity of those over whom they are established." And the same reasons that obliged men to submit to be ruled in accord with laws and constitutions equally obliged them to oppose rulers who designed their ruin or destruction.[32]

The theme of divine intervention in the establishment of government and in the institution of rulers found fewer advocates as time elapsed. The volume and strength of argument mounted instead on behalf of the Lockean interpretation. An essay in the Boston *Independent Advertiser* in 1748 elaborated on the theme that civil government was instituted by God "for the happiness and security of all." All men were by nature on a level, endowed with an equal share of freedom and with capacities "nearly alike," but each had a strong propensity to dominion. That, plus self-interest, made political society necessary. However, "there is no positive law either in nature or revelation, for any particular form." And the purpose of government was to protect the people and promote their prosperity, and any government contradicting that aim immediately left the people "discharged from all obedience" to it. A few issues later, the same paper carried an essay which summed up the matter: "What is government but a trust committed by all or most to one or a few, who are to attend upon the affairs of all, that every one may with the most security attend upon his own?" Another journal almost simultaneously announced: "It is an undeniable maxim that the first end and design of all government was for the benefit of the whole people."[33]

The pressure for a completely secular concept of government, and even a democratization of its purpose, found some clergy still unconvinced. The Reverend Samuel Philips announced in 1750, in an unequivocal statement, that civil government was "not barely a permission of providence, no, but an appointment of Heaven: The distinction of rulers and ruled is not the contrivance of crafty and ambitious men, no, but of divine ordination." From this followed the "unquestionable duty" of submission to rulers unless they "pervert their authority" or violated their oath and appeared as enemies to the civil and religious constitution.[34] But Philips failed to provide any hint as to who would determine such perversions or violations.

When Noah Hobart offered the election sermon in 1751, he took a similar approach, but without even the minor qualifications suggested by Philips. Civil government, he argued, was a consequence of God's permissiveness, and its nature required that there be men of different orders, some with authority to command and others with a duty to obey. The variety of governmental forms was perfectly proper because it was the result of differing "conditions and circumstances." The "original design and great end" of government was "public happiness," and therefore a man "must certainly have very absurd notions of the divine being, if he can persuade himself that God, in appointing civil government, aimed at nothing higher than aggrandizing rulers."[35] But Hobart did not suggest that rulers could be evil, let alone that a solution might be needed to that problem.

Some of the clergy by 1751 had begun to accept, at least partially, the more liberal conclusions of the non-theologians. A case in point was the Reverend William Welsteed. Although he could declare "that some bear rule over others, is certainly of God," and that "it comes to us with the most evident stamp of divinity upon it," he accepted the basic limitation of John Locke. While the authority and right of government extended from God, "the best right and title to power and rule over men . . . must finally be resolved into compact, consent, and agreement."[36]

By the early 1750's the secular viewpoint was frequently being expressed in public prints. A letter in the *Boston Weekly Newsletter* declared that as the "people are the source of all that power which is vested in governors for the public weal, they have an undoubted right to judge for themselves whether that power is improved to good purposes or not." This shift of the locus of power over rulers from God to man found further support in William Livingston's *Independent Reflector*. Communities, Livingston announced, "were formed not for the advantage of one man, but for the good of the whole body." Government "at best is a burden, tho' a necessary one. Had man been wise from his creation, he would always have been free. We might have enjoyed the gifts of liberal nature, unmolested, unrestrained. It is the depravity of mankind that has necessarily introduced government."[37] Livingston did not attempt to balance man's depravity with God's benevolence in the formation of government.

A counterthrust to this secularism appeared in the form of some "farther animadversions" on the sentiments of the *Independent Reflector*. "Some government, it seems then, mankind was under from the beginning of his existence, and no man was ever so independent as that he might do whatever was right in his own eyes. . . . Almighty God, the fountain of all beings, is the fountain of all power, too. . . . And this will of the creator is a law obligatory upon the creature without any compact of his own."[38] To this commentator, government was a divinely ordained institution, governors were similarly created, and man's only response was unconditional submission to those designated by God to rule over him.

Despite such occasional reverberations of the old theological view, the newer secular attitudes dominated the public press. In 1754 "Rusticus" ventured the simple statement that the "only true state of liberty" was the state of nature, but that mankind thought it best to form societies by first creating a constitution through a majority of voices. This was the origin of government. A theological liberal, the Reverend Jonathan Mayhew, repeated in 1754 that civil power originated with God, but he added that "it is to be remembered that this power is derived from God not immediately, but mediately as other talents and blessings are." No one form has His blessing more than any other—such ideas "are not drawn from the Holy Scriptures, but from a far less pure and sacred fountain."

Mayhew had made two significant concessions: power was derived from God mediately, and government was a "talent and blessing" rather than a penalty imposed upon mankind. And, he continued, as all governments were immediately man's creation, "so from men, from common consent, it is that lawful rulers immediately receive their power." We were bound to obey our rulers because government was an "appointment of heaven," but "it is not to be forgotten, that . . . law, and not will, is the measure of the executive magistrate's power; so it is the measure of the subject's obedience and submission."[39] Mayhew's capitulation to the ideas of Locke was complete, for he had agreed that the rulers were bound by law and that the ruled had the right to measure the rulers' actions against that law.

Perhaps the clearest exposition of the secular attitude toward the origin, nature, and purpose of government is found in Daniel Fowle's 1756 *Appendix*. He completely removed God from any active role in the establishment or processes of government. Political institutions, he declared, began as a means of resolving disputes among men, not as divine institutions. Governors were neither "the natural parents [n]or progenitors" of their people nor were they nominated by God, nor was their power limited by Him, nor had He described any plan for civil polity. Rather, a civil state was formed by three acts: a contract by each person for all to enter into a society, a decree of the people providing a plan of government for that society, and finally a contract between the people and those whom they had designated to rule them. Fowle dismissed divine right as "a mere dream of court flatterers," for if anything were divine it was the people's rights which were constituted by God and nature. The power of rulers was a simple delegation by the people.[40]

By the mid-1750's even the most rigid theologians were being forced to make concessions to these ideas. Moses Dickinson's 1755 election sermon is typical. Although he reaffirmed the divine origin of government, he had to admit, albeit reluctantly, the right of popular control—political societies "were not formed for the sake of the rulers, but rulers were made for the sake of the societies."[41] A further admission was made by Thomas Frink in his election sermon in 1758. He distinguished between God's direct role in instituting civil government over Israel and His failure to prescribe for any other nation. "Nor has Jesus Christ," he declared, "left any designed plan or model for the political government of Christian nations—nor doth God himself name and appoint the person who shall hold the sceptre." Rather, authority was conveyed to individuals or families "by compact, consent, or choice of the persons governed."[42] And, once the people's right to choose their governors was conceded, the means whereby they could call their rulers to account was admitted—the exercise time and again of that same right.

Although the Reverend James Lockwood could reiterate as late as 1759 that "the source and original of civil government, in general, is divine and from God," there were few clergymen who now took a similar view.[43] The role of God in the political affairs of men was, on the contrary, being denied by the clergy. The Reverend Benjamin Stevens, using as his source Burlamaqui rather than Scripture, defined civil liberty as "natural liberty itself, divested of that part which constitutes the independence of individuals by the authority it confers on sovereigns, attended with a right of insisting on his making a good use of his authority." Thus the subject who entered civil society retained the right to judge his ruler and to act as the occasion required. The magistrate must be secure in the allegiance of his subject, Stevens wrote, but the subject must also be secure in the protection of the magistrate.[44]

In 1762 the Reverend Abraham Williams went even further by denying God's responsibility for civil institutions and their operation. "The nature of civil society or government is a temporal worldly constitution, formed upon worldly motives, to answer valuable worldly purposes. The constitution, laws, and sanctions of civil society respect this world and are therefore essentially distinct and different from the Kingdom of Christ, which is not of this world."[45] When Williams washed his hands of the whole matter, he fully capitulated to the theory of John Locke.

Perhaps the best summation of the views of eighteenth-century Americans on this problem is in James Otis' famous *Vindication*. Certainly his statement is the pithiest: "1. God made all men naturally equal. 2. The ideas of earthly superiority, pre-eminence, and grandeur are educational, at least acquired, not innate. 3. Kings were . . . made for the good of the people, and not the people for them. 4. No government has a right to make hobby horses, asses, and slaves of the subject, nature having made sufficient of the two former, for all the lawful purposes of man . . . but none of the last, which infallibly proves they are unnecessary. 5. Tho' most governments are de facto arbitrary . . . yet none are de jure arbitrary."[46]

III

Religion and the State

GIVEN the background of the early colonists and their initial religious orientation, it is hardly surprising that the relationship between church and state was a matter of serious concern. Except where relatively isolated individuals like Roger Williams were concerned, seventeenth-century America seemed to accept some combination of the two institutions as a matter of course. The degree and method varied from colony to colony depending upon religious affiliation, but some form of church-state tie almost always existed.

Americans did not begin to question that unity and the right of the state to impose upon the consciences of its members until the eighteenth century. The passage in England of the Act of Toleration in 1689 certainly opened the matter to discussion by suspending laws against nonconformity for those who would take an oath of allegiance to William and Mary and disavow the Catholic doctrine of transubstantiation. By setting a pattern, this measure must have had an impact—although not directly measurable—upon England's colonies. Not only did it mark the first break in the traditional close relationship between religion and the state, but it opened the way slightly for a general discussion of the whole concept of religious freedom.

The first notable reverberation of England's action came in 1712 when the Reverend Thomas Maule deplored the conjunction of church and state in America. "The woeful consequence of this hodge podge mess of medley, and jumbling of church and state together again" had caused more trouble and suffering for the church than was ever known before. "Civil societies have their laws proper and peculiar to themselves, and the churches have their rules of discipline peculiar to themselves, and far different from each other." When the civil magistrate and the church "confound their jurisdictions under the law," controversy must result.[1]

Those considered nonconformists or dissenters within their local societies were most conscious of the problems of mixing church and state. The Reverend Josiah Smith, a Presbyterian, took up the issue in South Carolina in 1729. He suggested to Protestants that separation of religious and civil authority and the right of private judgment "are the only principles upon which we can justify our happy reformation from popery." If the first reformers did not adhere to those principles, what right did they have to leave the Roman Church? Yet, Smith alleged, the present Protestant clergy were denying the right of private judgment to those who disagreed with them, thereby unwittingly destroying their own right to maintain a separation from Rome.[2]

Smith's enunciation of the problem was soon echoed in the public presses of other colonies. Indeed, the question was being fully and openly considered by the 1730's, and the weight of stated opinion was increasingly in favor of the position taken earlier by Smith. An essay in the *American Weekly Mercury* asked with horror: "Is it not shocking that the same people who left their native country to enjoy liberty of conscience should turn persecutors as soon as they were in power? Yet this is true of many who went to New England (and I wish it were true of them only) to avoid persecution, and there persecuted the poor harmless Quakers merely for their opinions." Furthermore, Smith said, nothing could be "more certain than that persecution never did, nor ever can, make one sincere convert.

Are men's understandings to be improved or convinced by punishing their bodies?"[3]

Josiah Smith's approach is interesting, not only for his insistence upon separation of religious and secular affairs but because he is one of the earliest exponents of a great American myth—that the founders of New England sought religious freedom for all. This view, which does gross violence to history, was perpetuated through the nineteenth century and has only been dispelled in our own time.[4] Nonetheless, the mythology of New England's early religious outlook was being created, and Governor Jonathan Belcher used it in 1731 to flatter the Massachusetts General Court. "As one great errand of our fathers hither was to avoid all impositions on their consciences," he suggested to the legislators, "so it would well become the legislature here to make good Protestants of all denominations easy in their way and manner of worshipping God."[5]

Boston's neighbors did not accept the Bay Colony's profession of original religious liberty. A Rhode Islander, using the pseudonym William Freeborn, contrasted the happy situation in his colony to that of Massachusetts in 1733. The spiritual descendants of Roger Williams enjoyed among other advantages "liberty of conscience, which is freedom to worship God in the way we are persuaded is most agreeable to His will and most acceptable to Him, and which is the only indefeasible right of all men." Nowhere but in Rhode Island was this right "so fully enjoyed." Indeed, "we have even no terms of reproach and are burdened with no establishment."[6]

John Webbe, writing in the *Pennsylvania Gazette* in 1736, took issue with an author in the *American Weekly Mercury* who, after the sinking of a West Indian ship with the loss of thirty-two lives, reflected uncharitably that West Indians were vile, wicked, profane, and destined for general damnation. Webbe deplored unjust and unreasonable opinions such as this, and he then commented on religious opinions in particular: "But of all opinions, that which pronounces uncharitably of the salvation of souls is the most detestable. Hence arose all those cruel religious wars that have made such havoc among mankind for God's sake. When people's minds are tainted with such uncharitable sentiments, they make no scruple of destroying bodies whose souls they have already damned in imagination."[7]

In dealing with religious liberty in its broader sense, another contributor to the *Pennsylvania Gazette* said in 1738 that among the most dangerous men were those "who preach up . . . the doctrine of absolute conformity to a particular church. These persons would have us believe that the secular arm is bound to support them in their pious endeavors; though therein they make an open invasion on the charter of privileges, where the right to private judgment in matters of religion is asserted and granted in the strongest terms. If ever the civil magistrate (Good Heaven avert the omen) should lend them his authority, in vain should we sigh for liberty under a spiritual tyranny. History and experience assure us that bigots are of all others the most pernicious members of society." To censure persons for failing to conform outwardly in worship was blasphemy, because the forms of religion were human inventions, not divine institutions.[8]

The constant repetition of this theme in Pennsylvania was probably related to the hardening position of the politically dominant Quakers, who were fast losing their numerical superiority in the colony. But in Boston the need for protest was even greater, because the heritage of conformity was far stronger. The Reverend John Barnard devoted his attention to church-state relations in 1738, and he did so in the Puritan tradition. The situation in Massachusetts Bay was peculiar in that the Puritans had initially accepted the separation of the two societies, civil and religious, while retaining an invisible umbilical cord that was "the New England Way." The charter of 1691 had severed that cord by changing the criteria for participation in civil government from church membership to property ownership, but the memory of the past lingered on.

It was this memory that Barnard assaulted when he declared:. "When the civil powers shall take upon them to form churches, to ascertain who shall and who shall not belong to this or that particular church, and who shall enjoy the full privileges which, as members of that society, they have a natural and a religious right to, and who not; and when churchmen under whatever denomination shall pretend to exert an authority over other churches ... I say ... I must have leave to lament over our churches, with an *Heu prisca Fides!* and write upon them Icabod, the Glory of New England is departed."[9]

The same theme was discussed in the 1739 election sermon in Boston delivered by the Reverend Peter Clark. The secular magistrate, he declared, "may not use his authority to impose articles of faith or modes of worship on the consciences of the subjects, or enforce these by the civil penalties; for the consciences of men are immediately subject to God, and acknowledge no superior but Him alone." God shared his rule over conscience with no earthly authority. If the "magistrate's sword could pierce and wound the conscience, he might have a more justifiable pretension to exercise a jurisdiction over it." But it was the magistrate's task to preserve inviolate the right of conscience, for once that was broken into, "the sacred ligaments of society and government are at once broken and dissolved."[10]

An attempt to place the New England situation in clearer historical perspective was provided by John Callender, who published his *An Historical Discourse* in 1739. He wrote of the Puritan founders that they "soon discovered themselves as fond of uniformity and as loath to allow liberty of conscience to such as differed from themselves as those from whose power they had fled. . . . They seemed incapable of mutual forbearance. . . . In reality, the true grounds of liberty of conscience were not then known or embraced by any sect or party of Christians; all parties seemed to think that as they only were in the possession of the truth, so they alone had a right to restrain and crush all other opinions which they respectively called error, and heresy, where they were the most numerous and powerful; and in other places they pleaded a title to liberty and freedom of their consciences."[11]

But Callender was little heeded, for there was no need to dwell upon the past mistakes of the Puritans. The ministers of New England now argued for separation of church and state. Their motives, as Callender suggested, might be that they were no longer the dominant group, but the rationalization mattered not to the Puritan ministers. The Reverend Charles Chauncy, leader of the theological liberals, expressed the new view: "the use of force in matters of religion and conscience is not only contrary to the example of Christ . . . but to the nature and reason of things. 'Tis in itself a method altogether unsuited to work upon the minds of men. For whatever influence it might have upon their bodies, it can have none upon their souls . . . Force is proper to the body, reason to the mind."[12] Virtually the same thoughts appeared prominently in the Reverend William Cooper's Boston election sermon of 1740.[13]

While separation of church and state into distinct spheres seemed to be the gospel in Massachusetts Bay, it was not dominant in Quaker Pennsylvania. The Quakers' refusal to participate in the imperial wars and their political dominance combined to create serious problems. It seemed to many that they sought to impose their religious attitude toward war upon the non-Quaker groups. Governor George Thomas found it necessary in 1740 to reassure the Quakers that his insistence upon money for defense was not intended as religious persecution. "Far be it from me to attempt the least invasion of your charter, or your laws for liberty of conscience, or to engage any assembly in measures that may introduce persecution for conscience's sake. I have always been a professed advocate for liberty, both civil and religious, as the only rational foundation of society. . . . Religion, where its principles are not destructive to civil society, is to be judged of by HIM only who is the searcher of all hearts. . . . But as the world is now circumstanced, no purity of heart, no set of religious principles, will protect us from an enemy."[14]

Thomas' denial had little effect upon the Quaker-dominated assembly. But his suggestion of a practical limit to religious liberty found another advocate in Chief Justice Samuel Chew of Delaware in 1742. After espousing religious liberty, Chew added that it must be "taken under proper restrictions." It had "in common with every other species of liberty, this tacit condition annexed to it, namely, provided it does no hurt to others. In all governments the private ought to yield to the public good whenever they come in competition with each other." Chew faced the same problem as Thomas—the Quaker refusal to bear arms or support war. Chew suggested that such refusals were more in the character of civil disobedience than religious liberty.[15]

The conflict between civil obligations and religious scruples presented by the Quakers led to the publication of an essay in the *American Magazine* for January 1744 which was quickly reprinted by two Philadelphia newspapers. If the conduct of those involved in the Reformation was commendable, if they had a right to follow their own consciences and to repel all civil and ecclesiastical efforts to infringe that right, wrote the essayist, "every man, in every age and nation, hath an equal claim to the same liberty." As a "consistent Protestant," the author demanded that "every Christian hath an equal right to the peaceable and constant possession of his own principles, and ought to be left by all men, and secured by civil government, in the full and undisturbed enjoyment of them," even though they may be contrary to those held by the nation, by divines, princes, or the popular majority. Moreover, "every Christian hath a further right, to publish and vindicate by reason and argument his own opinions; to speak freely against all corruptions of religion . . . to separate from such communions and societies of Christians whose doctrine and worship he cannot in conscience approve of." And, he concluded, "as a consistent Protestant I do protest against all ungodly claims of spiritual men and all authoritative and coercive power in the Church."[16]

Chief Justice Samuel Chew again challenged the Quaker orthodoxy, and this time he did so more directly. He had penned a letter which several Philadelphia newspapers rejected for "prudential considerations." The *New York Weekly Post Boy*, however, printed the offending document in 1744. "New sects, so long as they stand in need of toleration, never fail to preach it up, and are able clearly to prove, that matters of judgment and opinion not being under the power and direction of the will, ought to be left free and unmolested to all men. But once established and confirmed, we too often find that those very people who have contended for liberty of conscience and universal toleration soon become more clear-sighted and plainly discover the necessity of uniformity in matters of religion, arrogate to themselves the right to prescribe to others, and even assume a power of exclusion from God's mercy those who differ from them in opinion."[17]

The year 1748 marked the practical end of public dispute on this subject in Pennsylvania, perhaps because it also marked the end of King George's War and the demand upon Pennsylvanians for men and military supplies. Also, the Quakers were soon to retreat from active participation in politics, thereby solving the problem which had given rise to these arguments. An essay appeared in the *Pennsylvania Journal and the Gazette* in 1748 which put a period to the controversial literature on religion and the state. Entitled "The Right of Private Judgment," the essay claimed that this right was the very basis of the Reformation. All efforts at imposition, violence, and persecution were "unnatural, inhuman, and anti-Christian." Private judgment was "one of those sacred and original rights of human nature which the Gospel had revived and re-established."

This natural right was based upon man's being "a moral and accountable" individual. Thus the rights of conscience were sacred and equal in all men and, since each was accountable for himself, his sentiments and conduct should be free and uncontrolled except as they affected the society's security and welfare. Man was given his reason for "a careful examination and free choice for . . . religion"; otherwise, rationality would have been granted only to the few who would lead the rest. "A man may alienate his labor, his estate, and several other branches of his property . . . but he can't transfer his right of conscience, unless he could . . . substitute another to be judged for him at the righteous tribunal of God." If the right of conscience not only had "signal advantages" but was natural and inalienable, it followed that no constitution or rule of society controverting this could be just.[18]

With the cessation of further commentaries in Philadelphia, the need to define religious-secular relationships shifted to the colonies of Massachusetts, New York, and Connecticut. In Massachusetts the crisis emerged from the Anglican Church idea that the Bay Colony was a field ripe for missionary activity. In keeping with dissenter traditions, this was viewed with alarm. The non-Anglicans foresaw all sorts of evil consequences, including the possible reincarnation of Archbishop Laud. Religious liberty now became a positive virtue for the Bay Colony, and its many attributes had to be well established before the evil Anglican influence made much headway.

The theme of "The Right and Duty of Private Judgment" appeared as one of seven of Jonathan Mayhew's collected sermons published in 1749. Those who discouraged freedom of inquiry and judgment in religion, wrote Mayhew, "are encroachers upon the natural rights of mankind, because it is the natural right and privilege of every man to make the best use he can of his own intellectual faculties." God directed each man to make his own inquiry, and whoever frustrated this threw "their chains and fetters upon the mind which (as the Jews said of themselves) was born free."

The question of the authority of magistrates in religious

matters was discussed in another of Mayhew's sermons. "I would humbly inquire how any civil magistrate came by any authority at all in religious matters; and who gave him this authority?" His denial of civil authority over religious matters was simple but persuasive: "It is evident beyond all dispute that the apostle in enjoining obedience to the civil magistrate had no thought of enjoining obedience to him in religious matters. For all the supreme magistrates then in the world were pagan; and idolatry was the religion by law established." Mayhew observed that the magistrate's function was "to preserve the liberties and natural rights of his subjects, one of the most important of which rights is that of private judgment."[19]

An anonymous pamphlet of 1753, which attacked the establishment of Congregational churches and the provision that their ministers be paid by the general populace, broadened the concept of religious liberty. The author suggested that there was no scriptural foundation for actions by the civil authorities to compel those who dissented "to hear, or pay for, such preaching as they apprehend to be disagreeable to the great end of the gospel ministry." It could not be founded on the rules of equity or justice, and such compulsion was "directly contrary to the example of Christ and His Apostles, and the practice of primitive churches, who neither used themselves, nor prescribed to succeeding ages, any compulsive methods to bring men to embrace the gospel."[20]

As the controversy in Massachusetts waned, a new storm rose in New York over the establishment of King's College and its possible affiliation with the Anglican Church. Dissenters feared this would lead to a further establishment of the Church of England, and the specter of suppression spurred the attack upon episcopacy and establishment. One author illustrated the dread potential of both evils in 1753 by commenting upon the situation of the Protestants in France, and then concluded: the "civil magistrate's power reaches only to the punishing of men for actions detrimental to civil society, not for opinions. Whilst men desire only liberty to worship God according to the dictates of their conscience, and in all other matters are willing to submit to the known laws of the land, no prince that values his reputation . . . will make a new law to entrap such men and bring them under the denomination of rebels."[21]

Much of the fuel for the public debate that ensued came from William Livingston's *Independent Reflector,* a journal established as a dissenting organ. Many of the commentaries in the newspapers were simply sharp reactions to some of the criticisms offered in the *Reflector.* "X.Z." prepared one such answer in an effort to demonstrate the advantages of an established church. He suggested that it could "diffuse, thro' a country, the full social advantages arising from religion." But his only reaction to the *Reflector's* suggestion that all religions be equally favored by the state was: "What a scene of confusion would thence arise!"

This same critic also saw political advantages to an established church. "The statesman has always found it necessary for the purposes of government," he stated, "to raise some one denomination of religion above the rest to a certain degree." The favored sect then became a balancing factor, keeping the others in subjection while they sought to replace the favored one and each therefore remained tractable. The true basis of British liberty, the critic insisted, was that no one sect so far dominated the others that it could afford to maltreat the dissenters. In this, he added, the English differed from Roman Catholic countries.[22]

Another of the *Reflector's* critics declared that "there is an incontestable argument to show that the Church of England is established here—for we are an English colony; and it is a decided case that every colony carry in their breasts the laws of the country from which they migrate, and are supposed subject to the said laws wherever they settle, till new laws to the contrary are made. . . . If there is no positive law to the contrary, the Church by law established in the mother country is the Church established here."[23]

To these apologists for an Anglican establishment, William Livingston and his friends responded with what had become a traditional American attitude. The only proper object for civil authority was something "injurious to the society, or some particular member of it." Religious opinions and speculations were prejudicial neither to the whole society nor its parts. "Matters of religion relate to another world and have nothing to do with the interest of the state. . . . The civil power hath no jurisdiction over the sentiments or opinions of the subject till such opinions break out into actions prejudicial to the community, and then it is not the opinion but the action that is the object of the punishment. For tho' a man entertained such opinions as would, if reduced to practice, be dangerous to society, yet while they be dormant in his breast they injure no man; and if no person is injured, no crime is committed."[24]

Although Livingston antedated modern Supreme Court decisions by two centuries, his early sophisticated position did not go unchallenged. "Aristotimus" argued that Livingston and his friends were scheming to bring all religion into contempt. "Aristotimus" rejected the whole Lockean distinction between a state of nature and a state of society and government. The state of society was "the true original state of nature," and God, at the same moment He created man, put him in a state of society and government and instructed him in matters of government and religion. "Is it not infinitely more natural and reasonable in itself, as well as more becoming a Christian, to derive the origin of society, religion, and government from God himself . . . than to derive it after the manner of modern imaginers, from I know not what imaginary explicit compact, arising from a long experience of the miseries of I know not what imaginary state of nature?" In ancient times the episcopacy and the magistracy were one, "Aristotimus" argued, and the rise of the papacy was an invasion of the rights of the princes. "I must think," he concluded, "that nothing can be wiser and better than our own just English constitution, which consists of a well-weighted establishment with a kind toleration." A similar attack appeared in the *New York Mercury* a few weeks later.[25]

Livingston responded to these efforts to toss aside Locke by admitting that certain laws of the mother country followed the flag, but only those which "are absolutely necessary to answer the original intention of our entering into a state of society." He noted that the colonies still extended the effectiveness of parliamentary statutes to themselves when they believed them to be useful and desirable, but he sharply differentiated laws for religious establishments. These, he argued, did not follow the colonists into new lands unless they affirmatively chose to utilize them.[26]

One of Livingston's cohorts, William Smith, Jr., took up the cudgels in the *Occasional Reverberator* and tried to develop a more spirited response to the Anglican position. "Britain is one body politic, but two bodies ecclesiastic," he announced. Everyone acknowledged the King as political head, and everyone fully accepted "the practice of [the] civil laws of our mother country." But Britain was divided in religious terms—part adhered to the Church of England and part to the Church of Scotland. Thus a traditional religious unity did not exist in the mother country, and therefore it could not be expected in the colonies. Liberty, Smith concluded, was an inviolable privilege of human nature, and while restraints were placed upon men when they entered society, they placed the restraints on themselves. "But moral liberty, or a liberty of conscience, is of another nature and cannot be transferred: It claims an entire exemption from all human jurisdiction, because its ends, offices, and interests are superior to all the ends of civil association; and subjecting it to the power of man is inconsistent with the very being of religion." Should government usurp this right, it degenerates into tyranny, and the right of self-defense becomes operative.[27]

A further elucidation of this theme was given in the "Watch Tower, #18," published by the Livingston-Smith group in 1755. Beginning with the view that "a lust of domination is more or less natural to all parties," it then suggested that it was stupid to entrust anyone with more power than was necessary. And "of all power in the world, none is so dangerous as power in matters religious." Once a man persuaded himself "that he is doing God's service by aggrandizing his own party and crushing others, what can restrain such a wild beast from committing universal desolation and havoc!" The anonymous author then promised to continue in a later issue with a history of Anglican persecutions in New York, beginning with the story of the Presbyterian Francis Makemie in Governor Cornbury's administration.[28]

The practical battle in New York was won by the Anglicans in the chartering of King's College, but the moral victory belonged to the dissenters who denied the funds expected by the college founders. Moreover, the dissenters got the best of the theoretical battle as well. As the controversy in New York diminished for the moment, the center of activity shifted to Connecticut, which still felt the aftereffects of the Great Awakening of the 1740's. This evangelical, revivalist movement, which appealed to the heart rather than the head, gave rise to a variety of new Protestant sects, but in Connecticut the old order dominated and the "New Lights," as they were called, were sharply repressed.

By 1755 most of the bitterness was gone in Connecticut, with the "New Lights" either returned to the fold or in the Baptist movement, but the very fact that Moses Dickinson

felt impelled to touch upon the subject suggests that some
unhappiness still remained. He acknowledged in his election
sermon at Hartford that year that a full discussion was not
practical, but he supplied several lessons from the controversy.
"No civil magistrate has authority to punish men for their
religious principles or practices, provided they don't disturb
the civil peace." Men's right to think and act for themselves
in matters relating to their own eternal salvation was "now
much better understood and more freely acknowledged than
formerly, when bigotry was too often substituted. . . . It is now
generally acknowledged . . . that all persecution merely upon
account of religion is an unmerciful violation of the law of
nature." Neither did magistrates have the right to make doc-
trinal or procedural changes in religion, nor interfere with
church discipline. "No external force, or violence," Dickinson
warned, "is to be used with men to keep them within the
church, any more than to bring them in."[29]

So far had Connecticut gone in the direction of separation
of church and state that a letter in the *Connecticut Gazette* in
1757 rewrote the history of religion in that colony. "Our church
and college were founded upon principles of liberty of conscience in religious matters. That same liberty our forefathers
enjoyed in their dissention from the church of England, and
would they, could they, confidently deprive their posterity of
the same liberty of conscience that they themselves now enjoyed and valued so highly? Admitting that they were Calvin-
ists, they thought charitably of others, they did not think themselves infallible, nor desire to bind the consciences of their
children. . . . Our forefathers enjoyed liberty of conscience;
shall we give it up?"[30]

William Hart three years later denied that there ever was
any effort to prevent individual churches from publishing their
own views of Scripture. "No man, I believe, ever thought of
denying them this liberty; nor even that of publishing their

sense to the world, by the press; except such as to serve the interests of error and tyranny, have attempted to restrain the liberty of the press. This liberty will never be denied to our churches; unless it be to enforce a regard and submission to some public standard of faith . . . to serve the designs of a party." In this, Hart opposed vehemently any effort to establish and apply an orthodox uniformity to all Connecticut churches.[31]

Complete separation of church and state, complete religious liberty, had so far advanced by 1760 that it was fully accepted in the home of Puritan orthodoxy. John Bolles could write: "the civil government as they exercise their authority to rule only in temporal things are the ministers of God, and that God hath not committed to them the government of his church, or to meddle in cases of conscience."[32] Indeed, the Boston election sermon of 1761, delivered by the Reverend Benjamin Stevens, expounded a doctrine which would have been anathema to a John Cotton or a John Winthrop: "the right of private judgment is inalienable—and since it is essential to true religion that we act from conscience and a conviction that what we profess and practice is agreeable to the divine will—religious liberty ever supposes, and it is requisite to its being, that the conscience be left free and that none pretend to an empire over it. Religious liberty supposes that there be not only free enquiry but equal freedom of profession and action, when thereby no disturbance is given to others." Stevens admitted the state's right to establish a church, but he reminded the Massachusetts General Court that "all such establishments are evidently human, and unless there be a general toleration, are inconsistent with religious liberty."[33]

In 1762 the Reverend Abraham Williams went even further in the Boston election sermon. "Human laws can't control the mind—the rights of conscience are unalienable; inseparable from our nature—they ought not, they cannot possibly be given up to society. Therefore religion, as it consists in right sentiments, affections, and behavior towards God—as it is chiefly internal and private, can be regulated only by God himself." Civil authority had the right "to encourage and maintain social public worship of the deity, and instructions in righteousness" only if it was "consistent with an entire liberty of conscience."[34]

From the time of Thomas Maule's observations in 1712 to Abraham Williams' election sermon in 1762, the American position on religious liberty underwent only minor modifications and required only modest elaboration. The basic definition held up well against those who sought an Anglican establishment, who hoped to recreate Puritan orthodoxy in New England, or who defended Quaker dominance and obstinacy in Pennsylvania.

The understanding that all establishments were improper had not yet been attained, but even that idea, too, had been expressed. The growth of a vast number of new sects and the fears of an Anglican intrusion sparked its development, but the creation of a true understanding of the absolute separation of civil and ecclesiastic functions remained for the future. Nevertheless, certain restrictive ground rules had been formulated for established churches by the 1760's. Forced attendance at an established church was not permissible, nor was the use of civil coercion in any form, and even forced financial contributions were coming under question. Any effort by the state to discriminate in favor of the members of one sect was also improper.

Thus to Americans in the eighteenth century the term religious liberty had certain clear meanings. It stood for the idea that while the state had a clear responsibility to produce a situation which encouraged religion, and might even designate one variety as the official one, it must not interfere in religious rules or discipline, it could not coerce on behalf of God, and it could not deny the benefits of society to those who differed in their form of worship. These attitudes underwent little change in succeeding decades and were incorporated in the new state and federal constitutions that emerged from the American Revolution.

IV

Constitutional Theory and the British Constitution

To COLONIAL Americans, perhaps no theoretical issue was as fascinating or significant as the nature of constitutions. They did not investigate the subject for its own sake but as a means of justifying their positions on purely local issues and petty problems unconnected with imperial concerns. Americans never sought a full and comprehensive philosophy of government, rather specific justifications of *a posteriori* situations. Having adopted stances in defense of this or that principle (as a means to an end), they could not logically disavow them when they became no longer useful. Indeed, through the year 1763 these principles remained most useful, and the continued recitation of them over so long a period gave them the qualities of an incantation.

Scholars have traditionally failed to understand the scope or depth of this view of government. R. M. MacIver, whose reputation as a political theorist stands high indeed, wrote thirty years ago of the American Revolution: "In America itself the speculative ground for this utterly unexpected event was unprepared. . . . There was nothing here from which to fashion the philosophy appropriate, indeed necessary, for the making of the new republic." But the colonists did not operate in a vacuum after 1763, a point MacIver overlooked. Even Alice Baldwin, whose study of the clergy's role is still a classic, did not fully appreciate the broad and long-term nature of the colonial investigation of constitutionalism.[1]

The years following the Glorious Revolution saw an increasing awareness by Americans of the need to define just what was meant by the terms "constitution" and "British constitution." Before the quarrel with Britain erupted in 1763, the colonists had reached certain clear and definite conclusions on both counts. Although the issues which gave rise to these debates in the public prints were transitory and are of no importance to us now, their results were significant because they created an American focus on the nature and meaning of constitutionalism.

Perhaps the earliest inquiry into the key question implicit in constitutionalism—the limits upon governmental power—is found in Samuel Willard's 1694 election sermon. His probe was tentative and his conclusions far from definitive. He noted that a great trust was placed in rulers and suggested therefore that "there is an answerable reckoning which they must be called unto." His sermon was the first indication that rulers had to account for their stewardship, but the reckoning was a divine one—"God sets up, and He pulls down."[2]

Fifteen years later Ebenezer Pemberton next dealt with this question in his Boston election sermon. This divine emphasized the varied nature of governments in the world but added that all fell into the ancient Greek triplum of monarchy, aristocracy, or democracy. But "where there is a mixture of these, where the powers of each are limited and brought to a happy poise, where power and privilege are so twisted together and inlaid in the foundation of the constitution as not to bear a separation without a mutual destruction; power can't be exercised but the privileges of the ruled must be maintained; nor privilege be enjoyed unless the power of the rulers be asserted and supported." Pemberton's means of enforcing limits upon power lay in the original contract establishing government, for "doubtless God has not left a state without a regular remedy to save itself, when the fundamental constitution of a people is overturned." But Pemberton failed to define the "regular remedy," or perhaps he was loath to be as rash as John Locke. Instead, he urged that "the doctrine of submission to rulers . . . [be] better stated and qualified on all sides."[3]

When Joseph Moss delivered the Hartford election sermon in 1715, he too delved into this issue, and he was the first to specify the visible limits of power. "All civil rulers have their power of government limited, and that by the boundaries of some laws that are the laws of that kingdom, state, or commonwealth." For Moss, the compact establishing government also established its limits, because "mankind never did nor will submit themselves voluntarily to the government of others their fellowmen, but upon some agreement of what rules, the ruler or rulers should observe in government." But, like Pemberton, Moss lacked the foresight or was too timorous to spell out the means by which these limits could be made effective.[4]

No matter how hesitant these Congregational clergymen might have been in offering solutions, they at least broached the problem. God's power of retribution was certainly one threat to overbearing government, albeit an ineffective one. Others offered more incisive answers.

The laity accepted the approach worked out by John Locke in his justification of the Glorious Revolution. "Cato, Junior," writing in 1733, recorded that "laws are no security, where they are not duly executed. . . . The constitution of the freest state and its most valuable privileges will never be regarded" by an emerging tyrant, "but will fall a sacrifice." No matter how "well and happily contrived" a constitution might be, its virtue and vitality lay in the spirit of the people.[5] Here was the first hint of the enforcement agency, the power that would make rulers hew to the terms of their contract—the people.

The limits imposed on power were the subject of a series of essays written by John Webbe in 1736 under the pseudonym "Z." He began with the flat statement that if government failed to attain the ends for which it was created, "the compact is void, *frustratione finis,* as the lawyers phrase it." The sole judges of this were the people. Their right to protect themselves by force if need be was based upon the belief that "no contract can tie up the hands of a people from repelling wrongs received from a prince conditionally chosen." Moreover, the people always reserved to themselves the right to alter the basic laws —the contract—as circumstances warranted.[6] Webbe had put clearly the basic ideas of John Locke. Others had previously used them, but with sufficient circumlocution to dull their naked impact. Webbe's directness forced the ideas into the open.

Neither Webbe nor Locke had much influence on the clergy at this time, for they continually shied away from this aspect of Lockean theory. Alice Baldwin has perhaps given the clergy more credit for *avant-garde* interpretations than they deserve at this early period.[7] While they did accept the idea of the contractual nature of constitutionalism, they consistently refused to accept the consequences of such a definition. James Allen's 1744 election sermon was a case in point: "Since the power of the civil ruler flows from the constitution he is under, the natural extent of it is limited by the maxim of doing that which is just and right to all under that constitution." Three years later, Charles Chauncy offered a more detailed but equally vague explanation in his election sermon:

Whatever power any are invested with, 'tis delegated to them according to some civil constitution. And this, so long as it remains the constitution, they are bound in justice to conform themselves to . . . Especially is this an important point of justice where the constitution is branched into several parts, and the power originally lodged in it is divided in certain measures to each part, in order to preserve a balance in the whole. Rulers, in this case, in either branch of the government, are bound by the constitution and obliged to keep within the proper limits assigned them.[8]

Both Allen and Chauncy suffered from the same reticence to discuss the means of enforcing the constitution. They could point to nothing stronger than principles of justice, either because they could not find acceptable means or because they preferred not to consider the Lockean approach.

This reticence of the clergy was not shared by the New York Assembly, which boldly announced in a remonstrance of 1747: "the same reason that obliges people to submit to governors and magistracy when they govern according to the laws and constitution of the country . . . does as much oblige the people to oppose them, if they design their ruin or destruction. It cannot be supposed that God, who has obliged mankind to preserve their lives, and consequently to use the means that are necessary for that end, should require people to suffer themselves to be destroyed or made slaves."[9]

Another voice was added to the laity's chorus when William Livingston turned to the problem in 1752. If princes "violate their oath and sap the fundamental constitution of the state," wrote the *Independent Reflector,* "the people have a right to resist them, because by that means they [the princes] put themselves into a condition of private persons and act with unauthoritative power. . . . They are to be considered as in a state of nature to have broke the original compact, abdicated their thrones, and introduced a necessity of repelling force by force."[10]

Later numbers of the *Reflector* spelled out the initial proposal in greater detail. Livingston declared it imperative that "a people should be careful of yielding too much of their original power . . . and always retain the privilege of degrading him [the ruler] when he acts in contradiction to the design of his institution." Still clearer was the statement that "in a limited government there are inherent rights and fundamental reserves. The resisting therefore the person or will of the ruler, when he rescinds those rights and reservations, is not resisting the Ordinance of God (which is the frame and constitution of government, not the person or will of the prince) but plainly defending it against . . . powerless, unauthoritative, and illegal attempts."[11]

Throughout eighteenth-century discussions of constitutionalism there was a silent but general acceptance of the wisdom of incorporating into the perfect constitution the three forms of government originally described by Plato and Aristotle. The magical properties of this political triplum—monarchy, aristocracy, and democracy—were first explained by Dr. William Douglass in 1749: "The concurrence of these three forms of government seems to be the highest perfection that human civil government can attain to in times of peace with the neighboring states; if it did not sound too profane, by making too free with the mystical expressions of our religion, I should call it a Trinity in Unity." A further explanation was provided by a 1758 essay: "Where there are three different powers in a constitution, and one of them desires to distinguish itself against either of the others, by a false zeal, the third comes into the dispute, with the credit of being impartial, and obliges the turbulent disposition to subside. But where there are only two powers, and no middle one, whose influence or authority can compose their feuds or compel them to peace, they run into all the extravagancies of faction and all the madnesses of passion."[12]

The character of the third force, the impartial power, was explored by an anonymous pamphlet published in Philadelphia in 1760. "The fundamental laws and rules of the constitution, which ought never to be infringed, should be made alike distributive of justice and equity, and equally calculated to preserve the sovereign's prerogative and the people's liberties. But . . . should the work stop here, the constitution would bear a near analogy to a ship without rudder, rigging, or sails, utterly incapable of answering the ends of its construction. For tho' the wisest and best laws were enacted to fix the bounds of power and liberty, yet without a due care in constituting persons impartially to execute them, the former . . . would soon become tyranny, and the latter . . . degenerate into licentiousness." The men called upon to settle the contests between liberty and prerogative "ought to be perfectly free from the influence of either," and "more especially" of the prerogative. This referred to a different third branch than that considered by other eighteenth-century commentators—the judiciary, whose independence was to be guaranteed by appointment during good behavior rather than during royal pleasure.[13] Here was perhaps the earliest hint of the idea of judicial review as an effective force in the preservation of the political balance in government.

The general theory of constitutionalism intrigued Americans in the eighteenth century, but the nature of the British constitution had a more compelling practicality for them. Given their own positions as members of the empire, it was important for them to understand just how that empire was managed. But beyond this lay another, more subtle need: only by firmly establishing the nature of the British constitution could the nature of their own governments be determined. The British constitution was the model, guide—indeed the rule for the appendages of Britain that were the empire.

Two general approaches can be distinguished in eighteenth-century American writings on the British constitution: one that it was a fixed and rigid collection of rules and laws; the other that Parliament itself was really the constitution and therefore continually subject to change. Each of these had major consequences for Americans. If the constitution were fixed, the colonials could hope to define the relative positions of governor, council, and assembly, utilizing Britain as their example. If the constitution were mutable and flexible, the colonists would be at the mercy of the governor who represented British authority, and their assemblies with all the powers claimed for them would be little more than air castles, subject to whimsical and capricious modification or destruction.

It is perhaps revealing that Americans did not begin to concern themselves with the nature of the British constitution until the 1720's, a period generally accepted as the real beginning of controversy over the growing power being exerted by the assemblies and, simultaneously, a time of increasing rigidity in the approach of Whitehall toward imperial administration. It was also a time of growing immigration to America from non-English sources. The colonists were beginning to mature, to identify themselves as Americans, and at the same time to grow more distant psychologically from the mother country. Thus there was a pressing need to understand the nature of the governmental structure to which they owed a certain allegiance and which played a key role in their lives.

The subject of the British constitution was first explicated by James Logan in his charge to the Philadelphia grand jury in 1723. He began by praising the British for combining in their government the best of the three forms of monarchy, aristocracy, and democracy, and then described the roles of each. "The king as monarch is supreme, yet limited by the laws, the power of which is vested in him, jointly with the lords, the whole nobility of the kingdom, and with the commons, whose representatives . . . are elected by the votes of the freeholders." Public justice, he added, "is administered by known fixed laws, which cannot be infringed or altered by the will of any man or by any other power than the whole legislature," thereby seemingly tossing common law to the winds.[14]

The relative powers and functions of each of the three branches of government under the British constitution continually intrigued Americans and served as constant points for analyses—which varied depending upon who spoke. The Pennsylvania Assembly lectured Governor Patrick Gordon in 1728 and firmly declared: "But of an English government, a House of Representatives is a principal and most important part, as being the main barrier of all those rights and privileges which British subjects enjoy."[15] But in the same year, when Governor William Burnet lectured the Massachusetts General Court on the subject, he stoutly averred: "The three distinct branches of the legislature, preserved in a due balance, form the excellency of the British constitution. If any one of these branches should become less able to support its own dignity and freedom, the whole must inevitably suffer by the alteration."[16] Significantly, Burnet's lecture was widely reprinted in the colonial press.[17]

Time and again the issue of the nature of the British constitution emerged from local controversies. John Peter Zenger's newspaper stirred such a discussion in 1734, and his respondent in a different journal plunged into an analysis of the weaknesses of the governments of ancient Greece and Rome, against which "Englishmen are sufficiently guarded and secured . . . by the happiness of their constitution." The key point was that "the property of the people is fenced, and the power of the prince bounded with received and established laws."[18] Another essay in the same paper, entitled "Thoughts of Pretended Patriotism and Publick Spirit," considered the reconciliation of power and liberty and concluded that the excellence of the British constitution lay in "that even balance of authority resulting from the mutual dependence of its several parts, whereby the power of the sovereign is moderated, and the liberty of the people is secured."[19]

An interesting feature of the discussion was the effort to date the British constitution. A favorite approach was the use of the Glorious Revolution as the point in time when the constitution, if not created, was at least made firm and definitive. "Surely no one will pretend to say," wrote one essayist, "that we enjoyed . . . liberty in general, in the same extent we do now, before the revolution; it was then that . . . our liberties and constitution were secured and established upon a firm and lasting foundation, and from that great and happy epoch we do and ought most properly to date the original of our present happy constitution."[20]

Regardless of the antiquity of the document itself, the theme of its fixed and finite limits on power was repeatedly mentioned by American writers. The Corporation of the City of New York in 1735 found solace in the thought that "the sovereign himself is tied down and restrained from doing evil." That restraint "is the most shining jewel, the most glorious attribute of our constitution, which prescribes the rules of acting, to the prince as well as to the people, and marks out the boundaries of his prerogative to such exactness that he cannot step over them without apparently encroaching upon the privileges of the subject."[21]

A vastly different approach to the problem was taken by John Webbe, who wrote in 1736 under the pseudonym "Z." Quoting Bracton, he began with the argument that "the king doth no wrong, for if he doth, he is not king."[22] Webbe contended that the monarch was bound by his coronation oath to govern according to the laws of the realm and to accept all laws desired by the people. His failure in either category automatically authorized the people to rise against him, but only Parliament had the power to determine when that situation had occurred. Indeed, "the power of Parliament is so great,"

Webbe continued, "that Burleigh used to say, they could do anything but turn a man into a woman." Parliaments were not only "the interpreters of the law," but no parliament could be bound by the actions of any of its predecessors.[23]

Webbe's theoretical position went contrary to that espoused by nearly all other commentators in this era. To be sure, his ideas were closer to the truth of actual practice, but this was not something Americans could accept. Their development of a more fanciful, structured constitution was a direct out-growth of their own needs. With American legislatures con-stantly grasping for more power and seeking to curb the royal and proprietary governors, a clear need existed for a frame of reference acceptable to all right-thinking men. Had Americans utilized Webbe's thesis and then contended that their assem-blies were parliaments in miniature, the English authorities would probably have been shocked into immediate and severe action. Thus the myth of a fixed British constitution served a useful purpose, for it permitted the Americans to set limits —in theory if not in practice—on the powers they claimed for their assemblies and so avoid the extreme ire of the Crown and its representatives.

Webbe's argument was dangerous, and his thesis of the un-limited power of Parliament came in for severe criticism from "Anti-Z" writing in the *American Weekly Mercury*. The sub-stance of this critic's remarks was that "resistance to the su-preme executive power is no longer considered to be legal but is subjected by all the authorities to the highest penalties." To "Anti-Z," the Glorious Revolution was simply the exception that proved the rule; it was not an event that could be used, as Webbe had tried, to justify future rebellion.[24]

One commentator took it upon himself in 1737 to analyze the "dark and defective history" of the British constitution. The origin of the three estates, he suggested, came "not from any deep previous thought, or original contrivance, but from the manner and circumstances in which the Saxons first took possession of England." The "order, discipline, and subordination observed in the army may, with great probability, be supposed the model on which they formed their civil government. The general was the first estate, the officers the second, and the soldiers in their collective body made up the third." A representative system emerged out of the difficulty of assembling all the soldiery in one place and at one time.[25]

Such fanciful analyses notwithstanding, the continuing need of the Americans for a British constitution structured on their own ideal pattern was evidenced time and again. "It is the glory and happiness of England," reported an essayist in Boston's *Independent Advertiser* in 1748, "that the prince is intrusted with all that is necessary, either for the good of the people or his own protection, and yet is so restrained by the fundamental laws of the constitution as that the subject is in no danger of oppression and tyranny. The rights of the people and the just prerogative of the Crown are . . . far from jostling each other. . . . No man in the community (how great so ever) is above the law, and the law is the people's right and property, and cannot be wrested from them but by their own consent. To resist the king when he governs according to the law is treason against the people . . . so likewise . . . [if the King seeks] to expand the prerogative beyond the constitution, or positive law, he ought to be deemed an enemy to the community."[26]

A series of polemical essays appearing in the *Maryland Gazette* in 1748 began exploring the various aspects of the nature of the British constitution. The first essay by "A Freeholder" asked the rhetorical question: "whether a parliament . . . has a power, i.e., a right to enact anything contrary to a fundamental part of the British constitution?" For his answer he cited British sources: "They say it is a vulgar mistake to imagine that a parliament is omnipotent, or may do anything for that they can't alter the constitution."[27]

"A Freeholder," having rejected the Webbe argument, then defined the constitution as "plainly an original contract betwixt the people and their rulers. . . . This was the case as well before Magna Carta as after it. . . . But whatever disputes may formerly have been concerning the original contract, there is not the least room left for any such since the settlement made at the late revolution, which was an express renewal of it. From that happy period our constitution has taken a new aura, not that the people acquired at that time any new rights, but that their old ones were more explicitly acknowledged and ascertained."[28]

"Philanthropos" in the same paper immediately rose to defend the Webbe thesis. "I take the basis, or foundation, of it," he wrote in speaking of the constitution, "to be the great law of reason, the rules whereof are deducible from the nature of things. . . . The dictates of reason, then, directed our ancestors to that mixed form of government that we now have. . . . I know of no essential or fundamental of the constitution, but parliaments; their existence was before the law, their origin cannot be founded in any law; we have laws for the choice and regulation of them, but not for their existence. An essential or fundamental must be before, or at least coeval to, the thing of which it is essential or fundamental. Now, if this be the case . . . they [Parliaments] must have an absolute and unlimited power. . . . Parliaments, then, are the very constitution itself. It would be absurd to say they can or would alter the constitution; that is, themselves. But there is nothing dependent upon the constitution, but what they can and may alter."[29]

As an attempt to evolve a compromise between the positions of "Freeholder" and "Philanthropos," a "Native of Maryland," in a subsequent issue of the same paper, inquired "what part of the constitution" could not be altered by the parliament? Was not every new law made or old one repealed an alteration of the constitution? He concluded that the constitution was but "a series of alterations made by parliaments," and the power of each parliament was always "as ample and extensive" as that of its predecessors. "Native" warned, however, that there were "some fundamentals which it would not be *safe* for a parliament to alter," particularly those that protected persons and property. If the legislature tampered with these, "the people would have had the same reason to resist . . . and to return to their original state of nature, and choose a new government." Indeed, the only area of parliamentary incompetence concerned "any of those powers, which by the joint consent of the community, in order to keep up their mixed form of government, the several branches of the legislature are invested with."[30]

"Americano-Britannus" concluded the Maryland arguments over the nature of the British constitution: "From what has been said, it will appear that parliaments are not the constitution . . . but that they take their form, powers, and existence from it. That they cannot alter that form or alienate those powers . . . without breaking through that agreement of the society . . . which constituted them."[31] Thus the concept of an omnipotent parliament and a mutable constitution was laid to rest in Maryland. It was an idea fraught with danger, and its unchallenged exposition could not be permitted. It opened the door to uncertainties for the colonies both at home and in England.

From this point forward there was no deviation from the American myth of the British constitution. Essays in Boston newspapers in 1749 and 1752 reiterated that the constitution was a set of fixed and inflexible rules. So too did William Welsteed's Boston election sermon of 1751.[32] The concept had proceeded so far by this point that the idea began to emerge that a law might even be "unconstitutional." An essayist in Massachusetts regarded a proposed excise law as "entirely unconstitutional, and therefore unknown, and never so much as once attempted in the English constitution."[33]

In at least one American mind, even Magna Carta became fixed and static. "This charter," wrote a correspondent to the *Boston Gazette* in 1756, "tho' it runs in the style of a king, yet it is not to be understood as a mere emanation of royal favor which the people could not justly challenge, or had not a right to before. For a great judge of law tells us that it is only declaratory of the principal grounds, of the fundamental laws and liberties of England. . . . So that it seems rather to be a collection of ancient privileges from the common law, ratified by the suffrage of the people and claimed by them as their reserved rights."[34]

Even the Act of Union of 1707 between England and Scotland was viewed in the same way. The terms of that act, a Connecticut pamphleteer declared in 1760, have been held "sacred and inviolable," because "if any act should be made inconsistent with, and contrary thereto, it would destroy the obligations to obedience." Not only did the British Parliament scrupulously adhere to the Act of Union, but so too did the courts. In explaining acts of Parliament the judges construed them in a way wholly consistent with the Act of Union, thereby suggesting that the American concept of judicial review was utilized by the English judiciary. The staticism of the American conception of the British constitution had thus led to the emergence in Connecticut, almost simultaneously with its appearance in Philadelphia, of an idea that was in truth uniquely American.[35]

By 1763 the Americans had certainly hammered out a clear-cut notion of the British constitution. In doing so they had been aided and abetted on occasion by royal governors and by the British authorities themselves who never bothered to contradict this notion because it also served their purposes. Perhaps "Virginia Centinel, No. XI" most succinctly expressed the established American position: "The supreme power is lodged in the King, Lords, and Commons, and measured out in such proportion that each of the three estates can put a negative on the proceedings of the other two." All Englishmen could rest assured because "the throne as well as the cottage, the king as well as the subject, is bound by these laws."[36]

V

The Colonial Constitutions

IN CONTRAST to the near uniformity of American opinion about the British constitution, a great diversity existed in the discussions of the colonial constitutions. This reflected the degree to which the views expressed in the public prints were colored by the need to serve local causes and solve local problems. Americans were not constructing a full philosophic system but pragmatically seeking to defend what they had already acquired, and to extend their control into areas previously closed to them. In both instances they drew upon theory as a justification, and, as before, found themselves prisoners of their own devices.

The debates over the nature of the colonial constitutions almost always emerged from traditional executive-legislative disputes and frequently dealt with money matters. The source of authority for government, the permanence of governmental forms, and the distribution of power within the existing structure were the questions usually under discussion. The answers varied depending upon the established form of government. It was far easier for an inhabitant of a chartered colony—either corporate or proprietary—to reach self-serving conclusions than for one who resided in a Crown colony. The first had a government based upon specific written provisions —a charter given either to the people in the form of a corpora-

tion or to an individual as proprietor—and he could point to
that document as a vested property right under English law.
The shape and form of the Crown colony's government was
determined by royal authority and legally subject to the whim
and fancy of imperial administrators. Thus the colonist operating under a charter had only to concern himself with a
definition of his government's relationship to royal power,
which he could derive from the document itself, while the
colonist operating directly under the Crown had only a royal
commission to his governor as a guide, and that was subject
to potentially rapid alteration or modification.

The Crown colonies' position was exemplified as early as
1711 by a dispute in New York between the council and the
assembly. The council, seeking to cut the assembly down to
size, announced that both bodies were "constituted . . . by
the same power . . . by the mere grace of the Crown, signified
in the Governor's commission." The representatives reacted
quickly: "the inherent right the assembly have to dispose of
the money, of the freemen of this colony, does not proceed
from any commission, letters patent, or other grant from the
Crown, but from the free choice and election of the people,
who ought not to be divested of their property (nor justly can)
without their consent."[1] The assembly's reliance on what
"ought" to be, on justice, indicated the weakness of its position. The representatives used this frail reed for a short time,
but they would eventually have to seek a stronger foundation
—the rights of Englishmen.

Later analyses of New York's precarious situation were
offered in 1734 by both William Smith and Joseph Murray.
These two eminent lawyers took opposite sides in the particular dispute but were in complete agreement on the premises.
Smith claimed for the colonists the "same constitution with

the people of England. . . . 'Tis very evident," he declared, "that we have but one king, who bears the same relation to all his subjects, as their common head and father, who deals not with one as a son and with another as a slave, but with all as children." The colonists therefore were to be governed under the same laws as the inhabitants of England, including Magna Carta and the Bill of Rights. "We hold under the same grand charter with the people of England: We have the same fundamental rights, privileges, and liberties as they have. Hence we have a right to choose the laws by which we will be governed. . . . Our American abode has put no limitation on these rights but what necessarily flow from our dependence; a dependence vastly to our advantage, which conveys to us the protection and superior wisdom of an indulgent parent."[2] Joseph Murray agreed with Smith's analysis. "Assemblies, or their power or authority," he added, "are not thereby erected, nor is their power or authority from that commission [from the Crown to the governor], but from the common custom and laws of England, claimed as an Englishman's birthright, and as having been such by immemorial custom in England." True, there was no "immemorial custom" in the colony, but as part of England's dominions, New Yorkers "are entitled to the like powers and authorities here, that their fellow subjects have . . . in their mother country."[3]

New York was not alone in the difficulty of spelling out a non-existent constitution. That New Jersey's dilemma was as severe was suggested in 1739 by Governor Lewis Morris' parenthetical comment to that colony's assembly when he spoke of "the King's letter patent, the only thing that establishes the constitution of government here."[4] Yet, when it served gubernatorial interest, Crown representatives were quick to draw the parallel between assemblies and the House of Commons. Governor George Clarke lectured the New York legislature in that same year: "Your constitution is built upon a plan as nearly resembling that of England as the nature of the thing would admit of; why would you not then tread in the steps of a British Parliament? Wise men make choice of the best examples for their conduct; you cannot have a greater or better, nor can your wisdom be more conspicuous, than in taking that of a British Parliament."[5]

Governor Lewis Morris found in 1740 that the New Jersey Assembly required still another lecture, and he minced no words: "We are a dependent government, and our laws (in their own nature) little (if at all) different from by-laws, extending no farther than our own province. . . . Nothing should be knowingly attempted in the least destructive of, or inconsistent with that dependence. . . . All governments that are so in their own right (of what form or kind so ever they be) that have colonies or governments depending on them, have a right, from the nature of things (while that dependence subsists) of knowing what laws are made by those depending on them, and of allowing or disallowing them."[6]

The New Jersey difficulties led to the publication in 1743 of an anonymous pamphlet, possibly written by Governor Morris, which spelled out the colony's constitution. It was "formed upon the pattern of that of our mother country, by virtue of his Majesty's letters patent under the Great Seal of Great Britain, and instructions in the said letters referred to, by which solely we have the power of legislation." At the heart of the quarrel was the question of the power of the council. Both the assembly and the council, noted the pamphleteer, had "derivative but not inherent powers." Within those limits, the assembly exercised the powers of the Commons and the council of the Lords.[7] Morris' difficulties with his assembly plagued him throughout his administration, and at one point he warned the legislators "that the calling, adjourning, proroguing, and dissolving of general assemblies is a power that his Majesty has been graciously pleased to entrust with me; and assemblies are bound on their allegiance to obey."[8]

No governor openly sought conflict with his legislature, of course, and when George Clinton assumed the governorship of New York he approached his assembly gingerly. In 1746 he urged upon them the idea that "every branch of the legislature ought to keep strictly to our happy constitution." Encroachments were to be avoided in order to maintain the proper balance in government. And he enjoined the legislators to "understand and love the English constitution."[9]

Sweetness and light did not prevail; instead, the basic power struggle continued, and within a year Clinton too became a stern lecturer. "Consider, gentlemen, by what authority you sit and act as the general assembly. . . . I know of none but by the authority of the King's commission and instructions to me, which are alterable at his Majesty's pleasure." The assembly, Clinton went on, "seem to place it upon the same foundation with the House of Commons of Great Britain. . . . If so, you assume a right to be a branch of the supreme legislature of the kingdom, and deny your dependence and subjection on the Crown and Parliament." The Governor warned them that "the giver of the authority by which you act, has, or can put bounds and limitations upon your rights and privileges, and alter them at pleasure; and has a power to restrain you when you endeavor to transgress them." Moreover, "every branch of the legislature of this province . . . may be criminal in the eyes of the law, and there is a power able to punish you."[10]

The assembly simply refused to answer Clinton's "inferences," perhaps because the virulence of his logic overwhelmed them.[11] But another such conflict in New York finally evoked a hesitant response from a defender of the assembly. Defining the British constitution as a rigid set of rules imposed upon monarch and people alike, the essayist said: "I suppose I shall be told that it is a piece of impudence in me to compare the plantations of America to their mother country." While not presuming "to compare an American governor to the King's most sacred Majesty, a council of the same place to the House of Lords, and an assembly to the British House of Commons," he reminded all concerned that only when each colonial institution strove to duplicate the merits of its English counterpart would the colonies flourish.[12]

The Governor's frontal assault upon the assembly's position evoked anger and stymied the processes of government. As a consequence, Clinton's supporters moderated their tone. A new defense of the Governor's position appeared in 1748 under the pseudonym "A Freeholder," and it simply announced that "the nature of our constitution . . . consists in the due balance between the several branches of the legislature." Too great a power in the assembly was as destructive of the constitution as too much in the gubernatorial branch.[13]

The anger on the assembly's side was apparently being replaced with coolly calculated deliberation. Rather than claim parallels between the English and colonial situations, the assembly now determined to emphasize the differences so as to gain its point—control over the disbursement of funds. The assembly remarked in 1749 on the differences between the Governor and the monarch, particularly where the King's interests were inextricably involved with those of the people, while the Governor's were not. Thus not only was the misapplication of funds more likely in the colony, but there was no recourse for New Yorkers in such an event. Therefore they needed a preventative rather than a punitive power.[14]

Cold logic, as exemplified by the assembly's remonstrance, could not easily be denied. Clinton thus had to fall back upon his original arguments: "no better rule can be followed than that which is given in the commission to the governors of this province (which is the foundation of the legislative authority in it) and the royal instructions which accompany those commissions." To give greater sanctity to those documents, Clinton added that they had been unchanged "ever since the Happy Revolution," having originally been formulated by those ministers "who distinguished themselves at that time by their knowledge of and zeal for the English constitution, and liberty of the people."[15]

For the moment the quarrel shifted to New Jersey, where Jonathan Belcher's difficulties with the assembly erupted into the press in 1754. He had sought to assign to the judiciary the exclusive right to expound upon the meaning of laws and consequently to determine whether or not a grievance existed. The assembly promptly announced that "our constitution forbids any such interposition in matters determined by our House to be grievances . . . for to suppose otherwise would be like a river rising above its fountain, and stopping the natural force thereof." The representatives sought English precedents for their view but mentioned only one from the turbulent days of Charles I's battles with Parliament. Belcher immediately challenged the assembly for its "search into the times of the greatest confusion, for a precedent to support such a proceeding; that House of Commons voted the King and House of Lords useless, and thereby showed that the whole constitution was to bow to the . . . House." And he further denied the validity of any comparison between the assembly and the Commons.[16]

By the 1760's it was clear, at least in the public prints, that there had been no satisfactory determination of the colonial constitution in the Crown colonies. A satirical essay appearing in 1761 amply stated the dilemma of the royal provinces:

The first thing to be attempted . . . is by an act of legislation to remove a most pernicious error. . . . I mean the absurd notion that we are entitled to the same liberties and privileges with our fellow-subjects in Great Britain, notwithstanding the distance of some thousands of miles from the mother country. This foolish conceit has already been productive of great disturbances to the province.[17]

The position of the proprietary colonies was much clearer. When residents of Pennsylvania or Maryland referred to their constitutions, they could point to specific documents which were vested property rights, an advantage not enjoyed by their brethren in New York or New Jersey. But complications in the interpretation of those basic documents developed in the proprietaries, and there was always the problem of setting the constitutions in their proper perspective. The permanence of the documents, the relationship between English and colonial forms, and the applicability of English laws in the colonies were among the problems discussed in the press.

A quarrel developed in Maryland in the early 1720's between the assembly and the proprietor. The assembly first denied the validity of the thesis espoused by the proprietary forces that Maryland was a conquered province and the people had therefore lost their rights as Englishmen. If it was conquered, they remarked, then the settlers were the conquerors, not the conquered. However, not even the Indians could be regarded as conquered, since the natives had sold the land to the English. Hence the colonists had not forfeited any of their English rights, and they were entitled to enjoy common law, English statutes, and acts passed by their own assembly. Since "the first inhabitants of the country were Britons, and many of them transplanted themselves at a great expense . . . they and their posterity should retain all the rights and liberties of Englishmen."

The assembly passed a bill to modify the application of an English statute in the colony, and the proprietor rejected it. The assembly responded: "What security have we of our English liberties and our properties but by the English laws?"

If these depended solely upon proprietary pleasure, then those who had transported themselves to the New World at their own expense had simultaneously abandoned their rights as Englishmen—plainly a *non sequitur*.[18]

The question of the nature of a colonial assembly arose in 1728 in Pennsylvania. One pamphlet asserted that the legislature in Pennsylvania did not have all the rights of the British Parliament because it was "of a quite different frame and constitution . . . so that no parallel can be made betwixt the one and other." The difference lay in the fact that the colonial assembly's powers were "derived from prior charters and the fundamental laws of the constitution," whereas the British Parliament antedated laws, charters, and the constitution itself.[19] This view was contradicted in another pamphlet which noted: " 'Tis well known, that the assemblies in these English plantations are formed on the plan of an English parliament. . . . Our assemblies . . . take their rules from the House of Commons." But the definitive word on this point was probably uttered by Governor Patrick Gordon in a speech to the assembly: "a legislative assembly in conformity to a House of Commons is invested with a very great authority."[20]

An anonymous essay in the *Pennsylvania Gazette* a decade later gloried in the fact that the colony's constitution differed from England's. "It is altogether as absurd to prescribe the same form of government to people differently circumstanced as to pretend to fortify all sorts of places on the same model." The Pennsylvania document was based upon Charles II's grant to William Penn, upon which the people "entered into a mutual compact for the maintenance of civil and religious liberty." That compact placed full legislative power in the hands of the people, and the execution of the laws in those of magistrates chosen by the people. Critics who "cry up the necessity of reducing the form of this government to the British model" were guilty of "a design almost as wicked, as was the attempt to change the English constitution into a democracy. . . . The thing is palpably absurd and impracticable." Above all, the essayist deplored any effort to enhance gubernatorial authority as inconsistent with Pennsylvanians' liberties; proof of the utility of the existing constitution could be found in the flourishing status of the colony.[21]

The question of a parallel between the colonial and British constitutions arose in Maryland as a consequence of a dispute between the assembly and council in 1740. The council wanted a long-term tax bill, but the assembly chose to follow the British example and pass an annual measure so as to insure annual legislative sessions. The assembly then took the initiative by attacking the authority of the council, noting in great detail the lack of similarity between the council and the House of Lords, particularly the fact that the councilors sat at the Governor's pleasure and held profitable offices at the executive's will. If the same situation prevailed in Britain, the assembly asked, could such a body "be called a free and independent branch of the legislature, capable of maintaining a just balance, or any balance between the prince and the people?" The Maryland council reacted by noting that the colony was a dependency of Great Britain. "But were we to come to a strict consideration of the difference between our legislative constitution and that of Great Britain, it would be obvious that it principally arises from the nature of a dependent and independent government."

At this point the editor of the proceedings interrupted to provide an explanation of the Maryland constitution. He agreed completely with the assembly's interpretation. The council was dependent upon the Governor and could not be an equivalent to the House of Lords. "By admitting the upper house to be a branch of the legislature a power is thereby admitted in the governor, who is a subject, to appoint legislators over the people, his fellow subjects, without their consent." The inadmissability of such a situation, the editor noted, was fully supported by John Locke's dictum that all laws must be made only with the consent of the people.

The editor's citation of Locke, however, was not intended to justify revolution in the colony. Locke's concept of resistance to usurped authority "is always to be understood as speaking of an independent society, above whom there can be no civil judicature on earth to which they may appeal when a tyrannical power is exercised over them. But the people in the colonies, as they live under dependent governments, are not justifiable in the use of violence against an evil administration because they have an appeal and may lay their grievances before the king or parliament."

The arguments for reducing the governments in the colonies to the model of the mother country held no appeal for the editor. The need of an equivalent to the House of Lords in the colonies did not exist. "Without them all the substantial ends of a British government may be obtained . . . with them the properties of the people will be dangerously affected." A House of Lords was desirable only "where any order like them have acquired an equitable and distinct interest from the rest of the people." Such was not the case in the colonies.[22]

The ever-present problem of money led to a serious dispute between Governor Robert Hunter Morris and the Pennsylvania assembly in 1755. The assembly followed the time-honored approach of claiming the exclusive right to dispose of public funds. Governor Morris' reaction was sharp and brief: "Your claim . . . is against reason, the nature of an English government, and the usages of this province, and you may as well claim the exclusive right to all powers of government and set up a democracy at once, because all power is derived from the people; and this indeed may be the true design." The assembly responded that it based its claim upon its charter privileges "to the rights of free born subjects of England." If Englishmen did not exercise such rights, the representatives admitted, then they could be deprived of them.

Perhaps more important was the assembly's closing oration, for it served to define the problem precisely. "The wisdom of the crown has thought fit to allow different constitutions to different colonies, suitable as to their different circumstances, and as they have been long settled and established, we apprehend that if the governor could have the power to unsettle them all, and make in every one such changes as would be necessary to reduce them to a conformity with his idea of an 'English Constitution,' the reformation would be productive of more inconvenience than advantage."[23]

"Pennsylvanus" wrote an extended essay in 1756 on the disputes between Morris and the Pennsylvania assembly in which he summarized the views of both sides. Some "say they have studied politicks in learned authors, and are convinced that our constitution is defective in these particulars; that the people have too much power, the governor too little; hence the lower sort are not respectful enough to the better sort; hence the laws are lax, and the execution of them more so." The contrary view was simple: the present system worked well and efficiently.[24]

To efforts to alter the Pennsylvania constitution, "Philo-Patriae" provided an answer with rhetorical flourish in 1757. "If then it be dangerous and destructive to the liberties of our mother country to invest a sovereign who knows no interest but his people's . . . with a power of making laws independent of his parliaments, how much more so is it to invest the temporary governor of a colony, a stranger to such sacred connections . . . with such an uncontrolled power? Deprive the people of their share in legislature, and what security remains of their liberties and properties! Their rights will be trampled underfoot, their properties dependent on the will of their ruler, their laws innovated, their constitution subverted, their liberty no more, and themselves reduced to a par with the meanest of slaves."[25]

The next dispute in Pennsylvania centered in 1758 on the assembly's power, granted in the colony's charter, to impeach. The conduct of Justice William Moore of the county court in Chester County came in for severe criticism from the assembly. The legislature sought to examine him and voted charges of impeachment, suggesting that the Governor, William Denny, could then try the charges. Governor Denny refused to acquiesce in the proceedings and announced that giving him "so transcendent a power" was wrong because the province was "so widely differing in its present frame and constitutions from that of our mother country." Impeachments were warranted by the usage of Parliament and customs of England, but the Parliament consisted of three bodies, King, Lords, and Commons, "originally founded in the nature of their institutions and the principle of an English government." The Pennsylvania legislature consisted of two parts only, the Governor and assembly. While the house could impeach, the trials must be conducted by the ordinary courts of law.

The assembly responded that the Governor alone sat as the equivalent of a House of Lords. "By the royal grant the governor and assembly here are constituted the two branches of the legislative authority; the one holding his powers under the crown, the other deriving their authority from the people; and a negative on our laws is reserved in the crown." The Governor, suggested the assembly, sat as a House of Lords "in an inferior degree," an idea rejected by Denny. "Power," he said, "once granted is hardly ever to be regained; and . . . could I think any governor or single man would be permitted by the British legislature to enjoy both the powers of the crown and of the house of lords in these colonies, you and your posterity might perhaps long have reason to repent the rashness of the offer. . . . That your constitution is defective in many respects,"

Denny concluded, "I shall not dispute with you, but undoubtedly this would not be the way to mend it."[26]

William Moore, however, did not find the Pennsylvania constitution defective. In a charge to the Chester County grand jury he announced: "The excellency of our constitution consists in the subordination of its parts, and the exact distribution of power for the administration of justice and wherever this settled order shall be infringed, and the powers of our juries and courts of justice parcelled out between the branches of the legislature, our liberties and properties will be at an end; the executive and legislative part of our government will be confounded into one, and our happy constitution wholly overturned and destroyed."[27]

A monetary dispute, one involving the right of the council to prepare a tax bill, evoked a final and definitive statement in 1762 of the nature of the Maryland constitution. The assembly refused the right of the council to prepare a tax bill for the lower house's concurrence and noted that the House of Lords never successfully assumed such power. The assembly claimed "the like rights and privileges" of the House of Commons which were "constitutionally inherent" in them, "unless it can be shown . . . that our dependent state upon our mother country . . . necessarily deprives us of any part of them."

The council reacted by stating that the assembly's claim of the powers of the House of Commons "will avail nothing, because having different foundations, no inference can be fairly drawn from the rights of one to establish the claim of the other." The Commons drew upon "a law peculiar to themselves, called Lex Parliamenti," based upon their own ancient usage. Simply to claim the title did not transfer the usage. "Your rights, gentlemen, are founded only in the royal charter, your particular usages, and the common law of England."[28]

Thus diversity was even the rule among the proprietary colonies. The Maryland assembly often found itself well served by claiming a parallel with the House of Commons while simultaneously denying any such parallel between the council and Lords or the Governor and King. In Pennsylvania all parallels were opposed by the assembly. In these two colonies there was clearly no overarching agreement on the nature of the colonial constitution. If anything, confusion reigned after half a century of debate.

Of the three types of colonies, the corporate ones enjoyed the most self-satisfied attitude toward their constitutions. A royal charter, having been granted directly by the Crown to the people of the colony, was not only a property right but was also one step above a proprietary grant. (While the latter were also property rights, they were issued to a third party, and the people consequently held their rights indirectly from the Crown.) As a property right, charters were nearly inviolable. Before such a document could be legally attacked, iron-clad proof of violation of its terms had to be judicially established. One consequence of this was the extreme difficulty royal governors in corporate colonies had in dealing with the people and with the assemblies. The *New England Weekly Journal* put it most succinctly: "Our charter is the great hedge which Providence has planted around our natural rights, to guard us from an invasion."[29]

Governor William Burnet soon discovered this truth. He had been a modestly successful figure as Governor of New York, but as soon as he entered Massachusetts Bay he discovered he was dealing with an entirely different brand of politics. The Governor's salary and the royal instruction to establish a permanent revenue for it initiated a dispute in 1728 which dominated his administration. The assembly was willing, on the basis of Burnet's reputation, to provide "ample and honorable" support, but only for a year at a time. The right of members of the assembly to make this decision stemmed from "the rights and privileges inherent in us, in common with other his Majesty's free-born natural subjects, which are in said royal grant [charter] particularly so declared and asserted."

Burnet's simple response stated: "The right of Englishmen can never entitle them to act in a wrong manner, and therefore the privilege in your charter to raise money for the support of the government is therein expressed to be 'by wholesome and reasonable laws and directions,' and consequently not by such as are hurtful to the British constitution itself, and to the ends of government." To the assembly, this would weaken the constitution by giving away "the great and almost only privilege" it had of controlling funds. "If we resemble the British constitution, as your excellency has done us the honor to declare, we humbly apprehend that no part of the legislature should be so independent." Moreover, "we have ever conceived that it was the peculiar distinction and glory of the British constitution, that every part of it had a mutual relation to and dependence on each other according to the different powers or privileges respectively belonging to each: Thus it is in the members of the natural body, and thus we understand it to be in the British polity."

The Governor accepted the bait and lectured the assembly on the similarity between the desires of the Crown and the practices of the British Parliament. The assembly immediately denied the parallel, because the King's interest was inseparable from that of his people's, but not so a Governor's. The assembly was willing to make its grant to the Governor at the beginning of each session so as to eliminate any suggestion of a pay-off, but it would not make a long-term or perpetual grant.

When Burnet illustrated his point with references to other colonies which had provided either long-term or perpetual grants to their governors, the assembly answered: "We are not knowing the motives inducing them thereto, nor the several constitutions of government they are put under, and thus this ought not to influence or prompt us to imitate them." The Governor soon lost his temper: "Rights and liberties are words that have naturally the same meaning in all countries, and unless you could show me wherein the British rights and liberties are defective, which you have not done, I may conclude that they are not so, and in that case it is a necessary consequence, that the methods under which they have so long been safe and flourishing are the most likely to produce the same effect elsewhere."

The assembly refused Burnet's logic. The representatives claimed that the royal instruction and Burnet's demand was an "untrodden path," that it violated the undoubted right of Englishmen by Magna Carta to raise and dispose of money as they saw fit and without compulsion, that it would lessen the dignity of the assembly and provide an imbalance in the colony's political structure, and finally that the royal charter gave them the authority to raise money as they saw fit.[30]

The dispute between the governor and assembly in Massachusetts Bay led to the publication of a pamphlet in 1729 devoted to this question and apparently written by one of Burnet's supporters. "We are a dependent government, and are incorporated into one political body by charter, and all our power is derivative from thence. . . . Some indeed understand so little about politics that they say, our general assembly have got a parliamentary power, and can do as they will; or as the parliament of Great Britain can do; but that is a great mistake. The parliament of Great Britain is a superior court, accountable to none but God alone. But our general assembly is a body incorporated by charter . . . and we have not an inch of power but what is contained in the charter."[31]

This clear analysis of the situation, published in the interim between sessions of the assembly, had little effect on the assembly's attitude. Nor, for that matter, did Burnet change his position. He again lectured the legislators on the parallel between the English and colonial situations, declaring that the royal instruction asked for something akin to parliamentary practice. The assembly promptly denied the parallel, restated its claim to authority over the disposition of public money, and argued "how insignificant the other branches of this legislature here must be, if an instruction to a governor must be a rule to the general court."[32]

The controversy which had erupted with Burnet's first session of the assembly continued unabated. He declared that it was not a rule because it was an instruction, but "because it is just and right." He also reminded the assembly that when it compared itself to Parliament it must remember that it was "subordinate to them, and accountable to them for your actions." The assembly denied the validity of Burnet's arguments and urged no more "controverting messages" between the Governor and itself.[33] The quarrel expired for the moment with the death of Burnet, but it was soon renewed under his successor, Jonathan Belcher.

Editorializing on a reprint of the debates between the Governor and assembly in 1730 over this same matter, an essayist reminded his readers: "the assembly of this province resembles our parliaments in England; the Governor represents the king, the council represents the lords, and the representatives represent our members of the House of Commons." He then took Belcher to task for threatening the assembly, a parliamentary body, with dire consequences for failing to abide by a measure projected by the Crown.[34]

The conflict broadened during Belcher's administration to include the idea that all funds allocated by the assembly should be disbursed only on warrants approved by the Governor and council. The royal instructions calling for this innovation provided that those officials would later be accountable for any misapplications. The assembly protested that this would in no way serve to refund the money nor give any relief, "for we cannot impeach, as is the usage of the House of Commons."

The only security was to prevent misapplication by controlling the distribution of funds from the very beginning. The charter gave the assembly this power, and "if an instruction may prevent or stop this, why not anything else? and so stop every act of government."[35]

The difficulties in Massachusetts had their repercussions elsewhere. In Rhode Island an essayist using the pseudonym "William Freeborn" reflected on the advantageous situation of that colony in 1735. "By our charter, our legislature and executive power are more agreeable to the equality of nature and do better serve the true ends of government than any other form or method whatever." The annual election of all officers led to a "Rotation in government which has always been sound and acknowledged the surest support and defense of a just liberty." An elected executive had spared Rhode Island the turmoil that existed in the Bay Colony.[36]

"Americanus" sought by means of a pamphlet to strengthen his Massachusetts compatriots' resistance to the threats and blandishments of the Governor, but no printer in Boston would accept it "for fear of incurring the governor's displeasure, which might prejudice them in their business." A Rhode Island printer accepted the job in 1739. "Americanus" announced: "The constitution, which you live under, is an epitome of a mixed monarchy, where your governors have every right to protect and defend you; none to injure or oppress you. You have a large share in the legislature; you have the sole power over your purses. But it depends upon yourselves alone to make these rights of yours, these noble privileges, of use to you. . . . Any compliance with an instruction which is contrary to the charter," he concluded, "is a traitorous giving up the liberties of their country, and an abuse upon his Majesty."[37]

The situation in Massachusetts had indeed deteriorated when Governor Belcher had to warn the assembly in 1741: "I would gladly have you undeceive yourselves and consider that his

Majesty is always virtually present in the General Assembly of this province by the representative of his royal person, his governor, and that by your constitution the king in this manner is the first and supreme part of this legislature, and without whom no order, act, or law can be made."[38]

As though to put an end to all these controversies, and to stop the gubernatorial heresies, Jeremiah Dummer's *A Defence of the New England Charters* was given its second printing in 1745, twenty-four years after it had appeared in Boston. This contained the most precise definition of charter rights yet given: "American charters are of a higher nature, and stand on a better foot, than the corporations in England. For these latter were granted upon improvements already made, and therefore were acts of mere grace and favor in the crown; whereas the former were given as premiums for services to be performed, and therefore are to be considered as grants upon a valuable consideration; which adds weight and strength to the title."[39]

Out of the furor in Massachusetts between the various governors and their assemblies came a clear agreement upon the nature of that colony's constitution and the relationship between the colony and the mother country. A series of essays appeared in the late 1740's and early 1750's explaining the powers of and limitations upon government in the colony. "A New Englandman" explored the issue of the security of a free state and concluded that it consisted in the preservation of a balance of power between the several parts of the government. He warned particularly against excesses on the part of the legislature which were particularly dangerous to the constitution. "There is no power in a free state independent of the law," and this he directed specifically at the assembly.[40]

A response of sorts appeared in an essay "Concerning the Civil Administration," which dwelt on the powers of the Governor. This was most revealing insofar as it described gubernatorial power in practical rather than theoretical terms, explaining that an executive in Massachusetts Bay had to achieve success through factional manipulation; it would not come to him by right. The essayist first defined the gubernatorial functions: he controlled the military and naval affairs of the colony, could suspend councilors or veto their appointment, nominate judges and sheriffs, and refuse to accept bills and resolves of the assembly. His really significant powers came from the political influence he could exert: since the judges, sheriffs, and militia officers were his placemen and had influence in the towns, he had influence in the assembly; he could recommend his friends to the house for employment as agents or attorneys for the province; and he could harangue the assembly, and often did so to the point where half of the assembly's journals were made up of his speeches.[41] The true source of immediate gubernatorial power, in other words, was not the Crown but was local in nature—something little understood by English authorities or by the governors themselves.

A minority view examined the concept of a parallel between the English and colonial constitutions and rejected it. The three branches of an American legislature, claimed an essayist in 1756, did not have a corresponding power with the Parliament of Great Britain. The idea that a colonial assembly had the same power as the House of Commons, a council the same as the Lords, and the Governor the same as the King "is absurd." Thus the power of the Commons was not a precedent for a colonial assembly. "The truth is, we are all of us British subjects . . . subject to British laws and entitled to British privileges. We are indulged indeed in erecting a form of government among ourselves, with a power of making laws, but this legislative body are always circumscribed by British laws, and . . . when compared with British Parliaments, are but as a shadow to the substance." The final proof of the subservience of an American assembly was its inability to make laws repugnant to a parliamentary enactment.[42]

But this was a minority position in Massachusetts. A much

more representative opinion appeared in the *Boston Evening Post* in 1761. After discussing the English constitution in some detail, the essayist claimed the benefits extended to "his Majesty's most remote plantation." The people of Massachusetts had additional blessings in the form of their own charter. "The house of representatives is one branch of the legislative power, so that the laws to secure our liberties, and by which we are to be governed, are of our own making. Nor can any tax be imposed, or monies drawn out of the treasury, but by the consent of our representatives. And the election of his Majesty's council by our representatives is also an article of far greater concernment to us than we are apt to imagine."[43]

The experiences of the three generic types of colonies suggest that the ability of each to defend its own institutional arrangements against British encroachments varied greatly, as did the theoretical tools each utilized. The position of the Crown colonies seemed little changed from the beginning of the period to its end. The battles continued and arguments went on, but the issues between the governors and assemblies were never really joined. That the political systems in the royal colonies operated at all resulted from an acceptance of the need to ignore the problem rather than any ability to resolve it.

In the proprietary colonies the issue was occasionally joined, but without any real conclusions. Only in the corporate colonies did the executive-legislative disputes lead to both an increasingly well-defined concept of charter rights, or constitutionalism, and a realization by the Crown and its representatives of the extreme difficulty of penetrating the colonists' defenses of those rights.

The unbalanced situation that developed, with some colonies fully able to state their positions clearly and find adequate theoretical defenses for them, while others continued to skirmish inconclusively, and still others virtually abandoned all efforts to develop a theoretical framework, meant that by 1763 the question of constitutional theory in an applied sense was still in flux. As the Imperial crisis deepened in succeeding years, it quickly became obvious that there was no common and local ground on which the colonists could defend themselves against increasing British authority. If they were to find adequate safeguards for colonial rights, they could not rely upon local constitutional theory but would have to appeal to ideas broader in scope.

VI
Rights and Liberties

WHEN in his old age Thomas Jefferson described his purpose in writing the Declaration of Independence, he stated that it was "not to find out new principles, or new arguments, never before thought of, not merely to say things which had never been said before; but to place before mankind the common sense of the subject . . . an expression of the American mind."[1] The Declaration's discussion of rights and liberties was certainly one of its most significant features, and it was this that Jefferson assumed to be "an expression of the American mind."

If Jefferson's assumption were correct, however, it was a mind that did not express itself until after 1763. During the preceding seventy-five years Americans were noticeably hesitant about spelling out the rights and liberties they claimed. Indeed, the *Boston Weekly Post-Boy* as late as 1741 begged the whole question when it charged its readers to

> Remember, o my friends, the laws, the rights,
> The gen'rous plan of pow'r deliver'd down
> From age to age by your renown'd fore fathers;
> So dearly bought, the price of so much blood,
> O never let it perish in your hands,
> But piously transmit it to your children.[2]

But Americans could transmit no more than vague generalizations. Only in dealing with the rights inherent in jury trials and the control of taxation were they at all specific, and then probably because these two areas involved continuing and pressing problems that had to be solved on a day-to-day basis.[3]

Abandoning specifics, Americans relied heavily upon the broad and undefined Magna Carta, claiming that its privileges were essentials of the British constitution and therefore followed the flag to the corners of the empire. In 1721 Jeremiah Dummer could sum up the rights of New England by announcing simply that "the subjects abroad claim the privilege of Magna Carta." When James Franklin was arrested the following year for publishing his newspaper in Boston, his young brother Benjamin responded by quoting Magna Carta and Lord Coke's explication of it.[4]

Americans developed a simplistic version of Magna Carta, as witness Isaac Norris' interpretation in 1727. The colonists, he argued, possessed those privileges secured "either by the immediate grant of the Crown, or by laws which the King himself or his substitutes have conceded to us, or by the common law of the mother country." Any denial of those rights by an individual made him "dangerous to the peace of the commonwealth." And, "when a man is injured, defrauded, or kept out of his right by another, means are provided for his relief by just and known laws and rules." This was what Norris meant by the phrase "Magna Carta."[5]

The question of who should interpret Magna Carta was involved in the controversy between Governor William Burnet and the Massachusetts assembly in 1729. The legislators claimed that the colony's charter and Magna Carta overrode Crown instructions to the Governor. This perplexed Burnet because he viewed the local assembly as subordinate to Parliament. Therefore, he stated, "it has a strange appearance that you should undertake to understand Magna Carta better than themselves [Parliament] when you know they are and will be your judges."[6]

Such attitudes did not hamper the colonists' efforts to use

Magna Carta to their own advantage. Its importance to them was most obvious in the area of grand and petty juries and the varied procedural rights involved in that system. "It is ancient and coeval with the first civil government and administration of justice in England . . . practiced by the Saxons," an essayist wrote of jury trials in 1733, and "confirmed since the invasions of the Normans by Magna Carta." Indeed, jury trials are "a thing of the highest [moment] and an essential felicity to all English subjects."[7]

Two prominent New York attornies, when asked by the assembly for their opinions on the legality of chancery proceedings, took divergent views in their conclusions but agreed on the fundamental principles of English rights. William Smith announced that the colonists were "under the same constitution with the people of England," and that all "are to be governed by the same laws." Thus New Yorkers had "a right to Magna Carta" and "share in the benefits contained in the petition of right" which confirmed Magna Carta and other ancient statutes. Smith concluded that "our American abode has put no limitation on these rights. . . . Hence we have a right to choose every law that is not repugnant to the laws of England; and to choose every law of England that suits our convenience; and to refuse every law of England that in its original institution was not intended to oblige us."[8]

Joseph Murray's rebuttal of Smith's position began by acknowledging the same fundamental principles. "I agree and join with Mr. Smith that we are under the same constitution and entitled to the same laws as are in England, and I shall beg leave to add what I suppose will not be denied, that as the laws of England are in force here, and the inhabitants of this colony have a right to the benefits thereof, that what is law and what is by law in England is and ought to be the same here."[9]

Another lawyer, John Wright of Lancaster County, Pennsylvania, emphasized the virtue of jury trials as he stepped from the bench in 1741. "Juries are looked upon as an essential felicity to English subjects, and are out in the first rank among English liberties. The reason given is thus, because no man's life shall be touched for any crime (out of Parliament) unless he be thought guilty by two several juries; and these juries being substantial men, taken from time to time out of the neighborhood of the person accused, cannot be supposed to be biased."[10]

An evaluation of jury trials, based upon common law and Magna Carta, appeared in one of the "Watch Tower" articles in 1755. They "are justly esteemed by all true Britons, as one of their most inestimable privileges. . . . It is undoubtedly the most impregnable fortress of our civil rights, which cannot be easily invaded without either abolishing or over-awing those incorruptible judges of matters of fact. And hence, we find the common law confirmed in this excellent bulwark of our liberties by Magna Carta. . . . With respect to antiquity, it [the jury system] seems to be coeval with our monarchy. Sir Henry Spelman . . . affirms it to have been used in England before the Norman invasion."[11]

Those legal procedures essential to English liberty were further defined in a letter to the *Pennsylvania Journal* in 1758. The author noted some "maxims of English liberty" which he wished the editor to lay before the readers "in conspicuous characters." No freeman was to be imprisoned or restrained without legal cause; the writ of habeus corpus could not be denied, and if the cause of imprisonment could not be properly shown, the prisoner must be freed; trials must be by juries of peers under the law of the land; and any power "above law" must be reduced by "every prudent and possible method."[12] But "of all the boasted privileges of Englishmen," according to the Reverend William Smith of Philadelphia, "the right of personal liberty and a trial by known laws is the first and highest."[13]

A writer in the *Boston Evening Post* asserted that the English constitution fixed the liberties of the people. "In England, the law is both measure and bond of every subject's duty and allegiance; each man having a fixed fundamental right, born with him, as to freedom of his person and property in his estate, which he cannot be deprived of, but either by his own consent or some crime for which the law has imposed such a penalty or forfeiture. And such law every man consents to by his legal representatives."[14]

William Moore, the county court judge whom the Pennsylvania assembly sought to impeach in 1757, reiterated the importance of judicial procedure to liberty. "The enjoyment of civil and religious liberty, the unalienable rights of private judgment, the security of property, freedom of speech and writing, trials by juries, and a government of known laws, not by the arbitrary decisions of those who may be our judges— are the things that ever have been deemed the great birthright of Englishmen."[15]

The universal acceptance by Americans of jury trials as an inestimable aspect of their freedom was matched by the colonials' dogged determination to retain full control of the power of taxation. As early as 1708 the New York Assembly announced "that it is and always has been the unquestionable right of every freeman in this colony that he hath a perfect and entire property in his goods and estate. . . . That the imposing and levying of any monies, upon her Majesty's subjects of this colony, under any pretense or color whatsoever, without consent in general assembly, is a grievance and a violation of the people's property."[16] In doing this, Americans were simply parroting the great lessons of seventeenth-century English history.

Much the same argument was used a few years later by a malcontent New Yorker, Samuel Mulford, against Governor Robert Hunter. "We have an undoubted right and property by the law of God and Nature, settled upon the subject by Act of Parliament, which is not to be taken from them by the supreme power without due course of law." Mulford's grievance centered about the Governor's effort to seize for the Crown's use all whales cast up on shore. To admit this was to admit the Governor's right to raise funds by his own fiat.[17]

A similar controversy arose in Massachusetts in 1729 when Governor William Burnet announced the Crown's instructions that he be given a permanent salary. "As it is the undoubted privilege of the English nation to raise any sum or sums of money, when, and to dispose of them, how, they see cause," retorted a committee of the House of Representatives, "and so hath been from Henry the Third, and confirmed by Edward the First, and ever since continued as the unquestionable right of the subject, so we hope and expect ever to enjoy the same."[18]

Out of a tax controversy in Maryland in 1748 emerged a classic discussion of British liberties. The legislature had authorized the county courts to levy a tobacco tax for current needs, but Prince George's County sought to use this power to raise funds for a new courthouse. A "Freeholder" complained: it "becomes the cause of every man in the province who is not inclined to give up those rights and privileges which secure to him his property from an unlimited power contended for in the county courts to tax what they please. I call it an unlimited power because the interpretation given to that clause of the act of assembly from which they claim their power is without limitation, and gives them the same power to levy five hundred thousand, or fifty million, as one hundred thousand." To "Freeholder," one of the distinctive features of British liberty, "the very soul and essence of it," was the right of the people or their representatives to hold onto their purses tightly and to be the sole judges of just how much was necessary for governmental expenditures and the manner of spending it. The same author added a few weeks later that this "is the great hinge upon which liberty hangs," and whenever it was weakened, so too was liberty. Only this could serve to control the great powers yielded to civil authorities.

The obvious rebuttal was advanced—the legislature had already given this authority to the county courts. But "Americano-Britannus" noted the great flaw in that argument: the people's representatives had only a delegated power for a limited period, and they were to return all of that power to the people at the expiration of their term of office. Having transferred that power to a third party, the county courts, they could not deliver back to the people what they no longer had. And since it was "a fundamental part of the agreement which constituted the society" that the people could not be taxed without their consent, this delegation by the legislature to the county courts was a violation of the contract creating the government.[19]

The universality of the right of no taxation without representation was best and most tersely expressed by William Livingston: "It is a standing maxim of English liberty 'that no man shall be taxed but with his own consent.' When the legislature decree a tax, as they represent the community such a tax ought to be considered as the voluntary gift of the people to be applied to such uses as they, by their representatives, shall think expedient." The Pennsylvania assembly seconded this in 1758 during a dispute with Governor William Denny over taxation of proprietary estates. "The right of granting supplies to the Crown is in the representatives of the people alone," they announced, "as an essential part of our constitution."[20]

Out of that same conflict came what was perhaps the most eloquent statement of the principle involved. "The king upon his throne cannot exact a single farthing of our estates but what we have first freely consented to pay by laws of our own making. We cannot be dragged out in violation of justice and right, to wade in seas of blood, for satiating the avarice or ambition of a haughty monarch. We need not fear racks, nor stripes, nor arbitrary imprisonments, from any authority whatsoever; or should such prevail for a time above law, yet while the constitution remains sound, we may be sure the very act would soon destroy itself, and terminate at length in the utter ruin of the projectors."[21]

There was an obvious interplay in the minds of eighteenth-century Americans between the concepts of liberty and property. An explanation of this relationship was provided in a newspaper essay of 1735. Essential for the well ordering of society, wrote the essayist, was to allow people the full extent of liberty and the protection of property. "As for liberty, it cannot be bought at too great a rate; life itself is well employed when 'tis hazarded for liberty. . . . As for property, it is so interwoven with liberty that whenever we perceive the latter weakened, the former cannot fail of being impaired." Indeed, if their properties were secure, this author alleged, it was difficult to persuade the people that their liberties were endangered; but if they were shown that their properties were precarious, "it is impossible but uneasiness and heartburning should then ensue."[22]

Americans handled the discussions of jury trials and taxation with ease and clarity of purpose, but not so their discussion of other liberties or rights. In 1725 the Maryland legislative debates were edited and published. These made frequent reference to the liberties of Marylanders, and at one point the editor intruded to familiarize the "unacquainted" who "may desire to know what those liberties are." He advised that "they are the same liberties that this province hath ever enjoyed, when right took place." For a "further and more particular satisfaction," the curious reader was referred to Henry Care's *English Liberties,* recently reprinted in the colonies. The House of Representatives in their debates had not gone much further in defining liberty, and one committee reported simply that since the "first inhabitants of the country were Britains. . . . They and their posterity should retain all the rights and liberties of Englishmen." Later the assemblymen resolved that "having the benefit of their English rights and liberties preserved to the first seaters . . . was one of the considerations of transporting themselves hither."[23]

No clearer definitions emerged from a controversy between the Pennsylvania Assembly and Lieutenant Governor Patrick Gordon in 1728. But in lecturing the executive, the assemblymen spelled out one point: "it is an inherent right, to be bound by no other laws than such only as bind them by their birth, from their ancestors as subjects, or such as they by themselves, or deputies, according to the common known rules of such conventions, agree to, of which rules the principle is, that the major part is to determine."[24] In seeking to establish the sanctity of majority rule, the Pennsylvanians suggested either a primitive, simplistic view of rights or an intolerable political situation in the colony.

Instead of a definition, the *Weekly Rehearsal* of Boston issued in 1732 a lyrical pronouncement on the aura of liberty, "the darling of a true Briton, and the peculiar boast and happiness of his country." The existence of this "darling" resulted from "something . . . distinguishing in our tempers that renders us impatient of any encroachment upon it, tenacious of our rights and willing to hazard all to preserve our freedom." The author was uncertain whether this distinction between Englishmen and others existed much before the eighteenth century, but he was convinced of its existence in his own day.[25]

However scrupulous they may have been to preserve their own freedom, Americans failed to define their liberty, to catalog their rights. Their refusal was based upon an eighteenth-century precept—that liberty was an all-encompassing absolute derived from the state of nature, limited only by man's positive action in joining society. Thus liberty required no definition, but that which restricted it—power or authority—needed limitation. Chief Justice Samuel Chew of Delaware first hinted at this in 1741: "Life and liberty, the immediate gifts of God, were common to all men; and every man had a natural title to an uncontrolled enjoyment of them. . . . And what is called estate, or property, was as absolutely essential to human happiness as even life or liberty." It was the attempt to blend liberty and property together that evoked the need for government and imposed restrictions upon liberty, but those restrictions must be carefully defined.[26]

The same concept was treated three years later by Elisha Williams. God had given man "a freedom of will and liberty of acting" restricted only by the bounds of the law he was under. In the state of nature, God established those bounds; in society, man created his own and thereby relinquished certain liberties. "The way to know what branches of natural liberty are given up, and what remains to us after our admission into civil society," wrote Williams, "is to consider the ends for which men enter into a state of government." But he concluded: "this I rest on as certain, that no more natural liberty or power is given up than is necessary for the preservation of person and property."[27]

Perhaps the clearest and most concise expression of this position appeared in an editorial prompted by the dissolution of the New York Assembly in 1747. "In all disputes between power and liberty, power must always be proved, but liberty proves itself; the one being founded on positive law, the other upon the law of nature."[28]

Given that framework, Americans had no need to define their liberties with precision. But they did describe some of the characteristics of their liberty, and it is from these that their meaning of that term can be pieced together. An essayist writing in 1747 noted its fragile and all-embracing quality. "But liberty, once lost, is lost forever, and the liberty of the most obscure member of the community, ought by the community to be as carefully preserved and as jealously watched as the liberty of the member most conspicuous for honor, wealth, and the other civil distinctions of life, because tyranny, like palsy, always first attacks the extreme parts of the body, but never leaves it till it has possession of the heart." Still another characteristic was the purity of the people. "Liberty cannot be preserved," suggested an essay of 1748, "if the manners of the people are corrupted, nor absolute monarchy introduced, where they are sincere."[29]

The best means of preserving liberty, granting that it was all-pervasive and that the people were uncorrupted, suggested one New Yorker, was the use of political parties. "Parties in a free state ought rather to be considered as an advantage to the public than an evil. Because, while they subsist, I have viewed them as so many spies upon one another, ready to proclaim abroad and warn the public of any attack or encroachment upon the public liberty, and thereby rouse the members thereof to assert those rights they are entitled to by the laws."[30] The essayist failed to say whether by his term "parties" he meant factions or parties in the eighteenth-century sense. To the mind of that day, there was a sharp difference, for the latter term carried with it the taint of treason.

Still another safeguard of liberty was knowledge. As Francis Hopkinson observed in 1754, "an ignorant people would turn liberty to their own ruin, inasmuch as they would be in most cases free to act, and yet utterly uninstructed how to act." Knowledge was indeed essential because government must be rational. It must be "most conformable to the equality that we find in human nature, provided it be consistent with public peace and tranquility." This, wrote a correspondent in 1753, is "what may properly be called liberty." And, said the writer, reverting to an earlier theme, liberty must reach to every individual, for if its beneficence were limited, it would be better not to have it at all, since it would only aggravate the unhappiness of those denied it.[31]

Americans clearly understood the conflict between liberty and security. The *Connecticut Gazette* carried an essay in 1756 noting that freedom was "a donation bestowed upon mankind by the Author of his being" and that it was "essential to his nature." But since every man had the same freedom, the "power of inferring truth and propriety from known premises," the possibility existed of his stretching his own freedom to the point of encroachment upon another's. At this point government functioned to restore the balance by introducing security. This same theme was developed more extensively in the *Boston Gazette and Country Journal* in 1756. Each individual received liberty when he received life, and he "has as undoubted a right to one as to the other." They were "both gifts of heaven— talents to be improved to the best purpose, and every man is accountable for himself to the giver." Entrance into society diminished liberty, but society was preferable to the state of nature because "there is more security" in the former. The liberties that remained "yet stand upon a broad bottom." They depended not "upon the wanton humor of a single man or a number of men," but upon "the Great Charter." It was "in short the constitution of English government—the basis of English law—the compact—the standing perpetual rule, over which no man nor any body of men distinct from the whole, may claim any just superiority."[32]

The constant evocation of Magna Carta, common law, compact, and similar phrases apparently served adequately to characterize the rights and liberties of the colonists until the imperial crisis of the 1760's. At least they were satisfied to continue the use of these catchwords without much variation throughout the period. The interesting question remains, however: what advantages, if any, did this imprecision have for Americans?

Perhaps more than anything else, Americans benefited from this approach by forcing the difficult task of definition upon the British. When specific issues arose, Americans sallied forth with a broad principle as their weapon, and the British found it necessary to respond with a definition of the principle. Often the American reaction to such definitions was simply to shift their ground and elevate an alternative principle, or to deny the pertinence of the proffered definition to the problem in hand. In this way the struggle could be prolonged indefinitely, and Americans often gained their point by simple attrition.

By 1763 Americans had made imprecision in the area of rights and liberties a positive virtue. In doing so, they accepted a basic eighteenth-century attitude as to the very nature of liberty and power. That this approach still had its appeal a quarter-century later was suggested when Alexander Hamilton, in Number 84 of the *Federalist Papers,* dismissed the idea of a Bill of Rights in the new Federal Constitution:

I go further and affirm that bills of rights, in the sense and to the extent in which they are contended for, are not only unnecessary in the proposed constitution, but would even be dangerous. They would contain various exceptions to powers not granted; and on this very account, would afford a colorable pretext to claim more than were granted. For why declare that things shall not be done which there is no power to do?[33]

Only when there was a clear and present danger—as in the case of jury trials and taxation—was it necessary to spell out the precise rights, the liberties, of the people. In all other instances it seemed far wiser to rely upon the contemporary concept that power must always prove itself. Such an assumption, however, would create an intolerable situation after 1763, when the British made a concerted and consistent effort to prove their power over the colonies.

VII
The Concept of Empire: A Fatal Flaw

LIVING outside of the realm but claiming the rights of Englishmen, Americans should have recognized that their position in the British empire depended upon an adequate definition of the relationship of the colonies and the mother country. Preferring to trust in the continued acquiescence of the Crown and its officials, however, Americans did not engage in extensive discussion of this problem. Instead, they allowed the English authorities to provide the definitions and, with but minor reactions, the colonials accepted them.

The reason for this lag on the part of Americans in the years 1689–1763 may well be the pragmatic nature of the people even at this early stage of their history. They were far more concerned with the workings of the empire than they were with its abstract nature. The theoretical locus of power might lie in Whitehall, but the practical locus seemed to be in Boston, New York, Philadelphia, and the other colonial capitals. There was thus little need to rebut the theories of dependency and subordination while Americans retained the ability to frustrate or at least modify the effects of Imperial policy. But the admission—at least by a failure to object—of these theories would severely prejudice the case of Americans in the controversies with Britain that erupted after 1763, and the rights of Englishmen so boldly claimed would be little more than air castles.

As early as 1689 a colonial official, serving in this instance as an apologist for Sir Edmund Andros and the Dominion of New England, defined precisely the subordinate role of the colonies. John Palmer announced that Englishmen "permitted to be transported into the plantations (for thither without the King's license we cannot come) can pretend to no other liberties, privileges or immunities there, than anciently the subjects of England who removed themselves into Ireland could have done: For 'tis from the grace and favor of the Crown alone that all these flow and are dispensed at the pleasure of him that sits on the throne." While some West Indian colonies had assemblies, Palmer admitted, "it is not sui jurie [but] 'tis from the grace and favor of the Crown signified by Letters Patents under the broad seal." Nor had Parliament "favored the plantations," but rather had always "plainly demonstrated that they were much differenced from England." The colonies, he continued, "are of the Dominion of the Crown of England, and without regard to Magna Carta may be ruled and governed by such ways and methods as the person who wears that Crown, for the good and advancement of those settlements, shall think most proper and convenient."[1]

Palmer's statement went to the heart of the problem created by the Dominion of New England, with its absence of a legislative body and government by executive fiat. Reasons for colonial hostility to Andros were obvious. A further elaboration of the position taken by the officials of the Dominion appeared in an anonymous pamphlet directed against Palmer's book. This author claimed that Andros did make "laws destructive to the liberty of the subjects" and sought to "erect a French government." Moreover, when people were arrested for refusing to pay taxes imposed without their consent, they were told "that the laws of England would not follow them to the end of the earth." The author further alleged that it was stated in Andros' Council "that the King's subjects in New England did not differ much from slaves, and that the only difference was, that they were not bought and sold."

Denying the validity of Andros' entire approach, the author went on to discuss an opinion of Sir William Jones, Attorney-General during the reign of Charles II. Jones had stated that the King could no more levy taxes from his subjects without an assembly's approval than they could discharge their allegiance to the Crown. "What Englishmen in their right wits," Jones had asked, "will venture their lives over the seas to enlarge the King's dominions . . . if all the reward they shall have . . . shall be their being deprived of English liberties?" Beyond this, the anonymous Bostonian inquired why, if the colonies were not part of the realm, did the government seek to quash the Bay Colony charter by a *quo warranto* issued as though Boston were included in Westminster in Middlesex, England? And finally, he noted that Palmer had forgotten "that there was an original contract between the King and the first planters in New England."[2]

Although this denunciation of Andros, Palmer, and the Dominion of New England was far from effective—certainly no alternate theoretical base of empire was proposed—more important was the destruction by the colonists of the Dominion itself. And the reign of William and Mary marked a return to the traditional outward forms of administration by governor, council, and elected assembly. Never again would a royal official deny that the colonials were Englishmen and entitled to the rights of Englishmen. Rather, a more sophisticated approach would be taken, and the question to be decided on an *ad hoc* basis was just what those rights were.

An illustration of this occurred in New York in 1707 when Governor Cornbury collided with an aggressive Presbyterian minister named Francis Makemie. The resulting case became a

landmark in church-state relations in the colony and was forever after cited by dissenters as an example of persecution by
the Church of England. At issue was the Act of Toleration of
1689, defining the rights of Protestant dissenters, and its applicability to the colonies and the effectiveness of royal instructions
to the Governor. Cornbury denied that the statute extended to
the plantations "except by her Majesty's royal instructions signified unto me." Makemie immediately challenged the instructions as either rule or law to anyone other than the recipient,
especially since the Governor was under no obligation to publish them and, indeed, was sometimes forbidden to publish
certain portions. When Makemie went to trial, the attorney-
general moved to introduce the royal instructions as evidence,
and, while the defendant consented, he commented that he saw
no reason for it since the charges against him were based upon
statutes and acts of Parliament. The defense attorney, William
Nicholls, summed up his case by stating: "I take this colony,
as a dominion of England, to be governed by and subject to
three sorts of law. 1. The common law of England. 2. The
express statutes mentioning the plantations. . . . 3. By the laws
of this colony." The jury acquitted Makemie, but once again a
prime opportunity to define the relationship of colonies to
mother country had been neglected.[3]

But Cornbury's difficulties in New Jersey, where he served
simultaneously as Governor, provided another opportunity to
define the nature of empire. The problem was similar in that it
dealt with the effect of royal instructions, but now the argument
was with the assembly. "We shall not dispute how far that
instruction may be a law to your Lordship," conceded the legislators, "but we are sure 'tis so to nobody else." Indeed, they
reminded Cornbury that "the last clause of the Petition of Right
. . . [requires] that the Queen's servants are to serve her according to law, and not otherwise." Any other approach would
be "not only a direct contradiction to the very nature and
being of assemblies, but must render the liberties, lives, and

properties of the people entirely" precarious.[4] Americans had again missed an opportunity.

Perhaps the clearest definition given thus far by an English official came from Governor Spotswood of Virginia in 1721. "I look upon Virginia as a rib taken from Britain's side, and believe that while they both proceed as living under the marriage compact, this Eve must thrive, so long as her Adam flourishes; and I am persuaded that whatever serpent shall tempt her to go astray and meddle with forbidden matters will but multiply her sorrow, and quicken her husband to rule more strictly over her." The clarity of Spotswood's prose was unfortunately marred by his failure to provide definitions for such key terms as "compact," "to go astray," and "forbidden matters." But his last sentence clearly suggested the dependent role of Virginia in the imperial structure, a suggestion not openly contradicted.[5]

"The extent of the laws of England into the plantations" was one of the issues in the famed Zenger case in New York. Lewis Morris observed that it was "a question often debated, but never satisfactorily resolved." His conclusion was an admission of his and his fellow lawyers' failure: the whole matter "has long been a sort of moot point."[6]

The non-lawyer was not bothered by the complexities that disturbed such a man as Lewis Morris. "A Truman," writing a newspaper essay in 1735, declared: "I think it is an undeniable truth, that as soon as an English colony is settled, the constitution of its mother country is to be observed as near as may be, for its rule and government." To apply the stock phrase "constitution" as the answer meant to drag in the whole American attitude toward constitutionalism. But since this American attitude did not jibe with the British view, no real answer, no real definition was provided by "A Truman."[7]

While serving as Governor of New Jersey in 1745, Lewis Morris restated his earlier position but with much greater clarity. At issue was the power of the assembly to issue paper currency and that body's claim of constitutional authority for such emission. Morris warned the legislature that "a British Parliament can abolish any constitution in the plantations that they deem inconvenient or disadvantageous to the trade of the nation, or otherwise, without being said to encroach; all encroachments being in their own nature supposed to be illegal, which could not be said of an act of a British Parliament with any decency, by any persons that understood what they said."[8]

Governor George Clinton also had difficulties with his assembly in New York, and in 1748 he admonished his legislature: "You seem to place the dernier resort in all disputes between your governor and you, in the populace; how his Majesty may take this, or how a Parliament of Great Britain may take your claiming, not only the privileges of Parliament, but privileges far beyond what any House of Commons ever claimed, deserves your most serious consideration."[9]

An extended analysis of the distribution of power both between England and the colonies and within each colony was furnished by Dr. William Douglass' historical treatise first published in Boston in 1749. He began with a distinction between the terms "colony" and "province," noting that the English settlements were more properly designated colonies, because province denoted a conquered people whose government was imposed upon them; colonies "are formed of a national people . . . transported to form a settlement." This distinction notwithstanding, the locus of power was Parliament —"the vacating of all charter and proprietary governments is not the ultimate chastisement that may be used with delinquent colonies; the Parliament of Great Britain may abridge them of many valuable privileges which they enjoy at present; as happened in an affair relating to Ireland in 1720. . . . Therefore the colonies ought to be circumspect and not offend their mother country."[10]

This view of colonial dependency and subjection was not restricted to those who held office under the Crown, as witness Douglass' pointed remarks. "Zacharius Plaintruth," writing in 1752, warned his fellow New Yorkers: "you live under a form of government, that at first glance, has the resemblance of the English constitution; but in sober sadness, my friend, you are not the shadow of it; you are not aware perhaps, of the word prerogative, or the significations of it, though by that alone you are ruled; you don't seem to understand that the royal pleasure is your Magna Carta; tho' as yet, by the sole indulgence of our princes (and, methinks it should be a weighty argument, to excite your loyalty and gratitude), you are equally happy with those [the English] who obtained theirs with a vast expense of blood and treasure." Should further clarity be needed, the author concluded: "you are new clay in the potter's hand, and whenever you shall be placed upon his wheel, the wisest of you all can't tell in what figure you are designed to be taken off."[11]

On occasion, when it suited their purposes, Americans even denied the validity of the extension of English laws to the colonies, thereby giving further substance to the theory of a second-class citizenship in the empire, though this was not necessarily their intention. In the midst of the debate over King's College in New York in the 1750's, the Livingston dissenter group denied the extension of common law to New York because it was a conquered province. This, of course, scuttled the argument that the Church of England was established in the colony because it was established in England by common law, but it left the colony wide open to far more serious problems.

The dissenters in New York went so far as to quote Sir John Randolph, a Virginia lawyer and an Anglican, to buttress their position that common law and statute law did not automatically follow the flag. "If we wade into the statutes," wrote

Randolph, "no man can tell what the law is. It is certain all of them cannot bind, and to know which do was always above my capacity." Even those statutes declaratory of common law, he added, were simply illustrative rather than binding in and of themselves.[12]

The confusion that bothered Randolph also perplexed Archibald Kennedy, who argued against an Anglican establishment in New York. He averred "that wherever colonies issue, whether by conquest or otherwise, the laws of that country from whence they have their existence, being their birthright, are, and must be in force till other laws are given them." On this basis he claimed that English common and statute law had been introduced into New York for the protection of property, but somehow he distinguished between laws for such purposes and those for the establishment of the Church of England. The latter, he insisted, had not been introduced.[13]

New Yorkers were reminded again in 1761 by Governor Cadwallader Colden of the fragility of their position. While assuring the assembly of his intention to concur in all measures for "the benefit of the country," he warned them that they were "a small dependent state" and cautioned against any "attempt to set bounds to and restrain the rights and prerogatives of the King of Great Britain."[14] A frail rebuttal appeared in the following year with a newspaper essay claiming that "when a nation takes possession of a distant country, and settles a colony there, that country, though separated from the principal establishment or mother country, naturally becomes a part of the state equally with its ancient possessions, and is entitled to the same laws and privileges."[15]

Embers of the earlier controversy created by Sir Edmund Andros and the Dominion of New England were stirred up again by the crisis over the Writs of Assistance in Boston. An essay recalled that "the people of the province formerly . . . asserted the rights of Englishmen: And they did it with a sober, manly spirit: They were then in an insulting manner asked 'whether English rights were to follow them to the ends of the earth.' " Three-quarters of a century later, New Englanders were being told "that the rights we contend for 'do not belong to the English.' " All that the essayist could respond was: "we desire no securities but such as are derived to us from the British constitution, which is our glory—no laws but what are agreeable to the true spirit of the British laws."[16]

Americans had clearly ignored throughout the eighteenth century the vital problem of the locus of power. Perhaps it would have been too dangerous to tackle, though certainly this was one of the key issues that would dominate political arguments in the years after 1763, when it was far more dangerous to consider such matters. Perhaps, had they forthrightly approached this issue earlier and reached a conclusion, it would have been less difficult to secure acquiescence in it after 1763. Such wishful thinking aside, it is clear that Americans had forfeited all of the other definitions so carefully enunciated throughout this period by their failure to consider the locus of power.

VIII
The Ideological Discontinuity

ALL TOO often historians have viewed the years before 1763 as part of a continuous flow toward the American Revolution, as a mere prelude to the grand collapse of the old empire. A similar attitude toward the late Middle Ages bothered Johan Huizinga a number of years ago, and he demonstrated that the fourteenth and fifteenth centuries were more important as the culmination of medievalism than as the birth of the Enlightenment. Somewhat later, Carl Becker attempted the same thing for the Enlightenment, demonstrating that its ties with the Middle Ages were stronger than with the nineteenth century.[1]

The same point can be made about the years 1689–1763 in American history. Certainly in the area of political ideology, which only recently has come under extensive study, the tendency already exists of looking at political thought as a progressive unfolding of ideas which move with only minor disruptions from the Mayflower Compact to the Declaration of Independence and the Constitution. But it is closer to truth to assert that Americans by 1763 were nearer the Mayflower Compact in their thought than the events of 1776, that they had no idea of independence and were even repelled by it. Whatever shape their ideology had taken by the end of the French and Indian War, it was molded by the British Empire as they knew and accepted it.

Viewed in the light of the demands of 1776, American ideology thirteen years earlier was certainly ill-informed, full of gaps, and inadequate as a tool. But for the purposes of 1763 it was perfectly satisfactory. A recent analyst, having looked at the years before 1763, concluded that there was no clear ideology. He then proceeded to explain this phenomenon by arguing that the institutional system worked so well that there was no need to theorize about it. Thus to understand the unspoken (or unwritten) ideology, he suggested, one must find it in the workings of the institutions themselves.[2]

This view can be challenged on two grounds. First, it is ahistorical. It approaches the period with a preconceived notion —that there should be a revolutionary ideology—and having found no evidence for it, seeks an explanation for the colonials' grievous oversight. Second, despite the author's failure to find it, a political ideology had been developed and expressed, but it was not revolutionary. A direct, clear, and simple line cannot be drawn between the thought of 1763 and 1776.

American political ideology emerged in these years of the eighteenth century from a series of crises, some minor and some of larger significance, in almost every mainland colony. Each colony had its own peculiar problems, but at the root of every one were certain basic similarities. From the diversity of local difficulties emerged a generally uniform response, an ideology which met the needs of Americans in more than one locality. The constant reprinting of political essays by newspapers in different colonies suggests the wide appeal of this ideology.

At the core of the ideological discussion was the development of freedom of the press as a viable concept. Without it there could be no free exchange of ideas on governmental problems. It emerged hesitantly, but by the time of Zenger's trial, newspapers were openly proclaiming it. Like any freedom, it was not absolute in its initial stages, but the wider its support, the stronger its definition became. By the 1760's its existence was undeniable and it was absolute in nature. Indeed, the whole revolutionary movement could not have occurred without it. After 1763 royal authorities bewailed their inability to control criticism, to curb the press—in Massachusetts the Tories referred to the *Boston Gazette* as the "Weekly Dung Barge," but they could not curtail its output.[3]

Americans tackled the problem of political ideology from its very roots—an understanding of the state of nature and the origin of government. Both topics were highly theoretical, indicating that the colonists had a sophisticated approach to the problem. They quickly seized upon the Lockean interpretation of the state of nature and echoed his view that it was a state of perfect and absolute freedom governed only by the law of nature. This idyllic condition was abandoned in favor of society and government only because of the difficulty of preserving each individual's total freedom.

The origin of government and its purpose and nature proved a thornier subject for Americans and led to greater disagreement. At first they were hampered by their theological orientation. If government was God's ordinance to man, little more need be said. Disagreement with government became rebellion against authority and, in turn, opposition to God—an unthinkable situation. Only when the clergy accepted the idea that government originated not in a divine decree but by compact or agreement among the people could Americans explore possible limits upon political power. Having done that, they moved easily to the thesis that rulers were bound by law, and transgression of those limits released the people from further obedience. This had noteworthy implications, and James Otis used them to the fullest when he announced: "tho' most governments are de facto arbitrary . . . yet none are de jure arbitrary."[4]

Removal of God from the origins of government also permitted removal of government from the concerns of religion. Many arguments were involved in the final realization that the state had no proper function in religious coercion, or any religious matters, but it seems likely these would have been fruitless without the concurrent agreement on the division of secular and religious affairs. Accepting the idea that man's relations with his Maker were a personal matter, that efforts at coercion of the soul or mind were valueless, Americans concluded that government's only function was to provide a situation which encouraged religion.

Agreement by Americans on these broad areas did not, however, carry over into some other equally crucial ones. Their discussions of constitutionalism suggested serious flaws in their understanding of its implications. Seeking justifications of *a priori* situations which varied from colony to colony, their responses were equally varied. Some argued for a fixed British constitution, while others contended that Parliament itself was the constitution. After extensive controversy there emerged an agreement that the British constitution was fixed and that finite limits were imposed on governmental power, an essential position given the nature of colonial political institutions and their constant efforts to expand the limits of their own authority.

But agreement on the nature of constitutionalism at this level was not applied at the local level. The variety of colonial constitutions led to sharply differing interpretations of what those constitutions were. Each colony sought to defend its own institutional arrangements against external pressures, but some began with greater advantages than others. The Crown colonies found themselves almost totally defenseless in theory—though not in practice—against royal intervention, while proprietary colonies had the advantage of charter rights—though these were once removed from the fount of ultimate authority—and corporate colonies were almost invulnerable from outside political forces. Consequently, Crown colonies made little headway in defining constitutionalism as it applied to themselves, proprietary ones succeeded a little better, and corporate colonies structured full theoretical defenses of their positions. Colonial response in this area, however, was so uneven as to force Americans after 1763 to seek new theoretical defenses against imperial power.

Inadequacies of definition were also reflected in discussions of rights and liberties. Americans made little effort to define these—except for the always critical matters of jury trials and taxation—because they relied heavily upon the traditional slogan of "rights of Englishmen." At first glance, failure to define their essential rights seems incongruous, particularly with all of the effort expended in other areas. But their attitude was based upon a simplistic truism—that liberty was absolute and God-given, thus requiring no definition, while power was a human creation and therefore required precise limitation. This, of course, was closely related to the whole Lockean concept of the state of nature in which liberty was absolute. Creation of government gave birth to power, and the very fact of creation gave it limits and definitions.

In addition to the theoretical rationale behind their view of liberty and power, Americans found a practical value in keeping this concept fluid and flexible. It forced those who wished to curb colonial liberties and rights to make the definitions. And considering that the external force most interested in offering such definitions lay three thousand miles away, Americans had a clear-cut advantage; the British were frustrated by the impossibility of communicating quickly and effectively with the empire's extremities. Nonetheless, the colonials lacked foresight, because their failure to respond adequately to the nature and meaning of their rights and liberties lost for them certain benefits that would have proven useful after 1763.

More important, they had not challenged the constant re-iteration by royal authorities and officials in America that colonies were subordinate and dependent, that ultimate authority was wielded either by the King or Parliament—or more precisely by King in Parliament. Such statements could be ignored as long as they emanated from individuals, no matter how highly placed. But when Parliament passed the Declaratory Act in 1766, the British position was most explicit and had behind it the ultimate authority of the empire: "The said colonies and plantations in America have been, are, and of right ought to be subordinate unto, and dependent upon the imperial crown and parliament of Great Britain; and that the King's majesty, by and with the advice and consent of the lords spiritual and temporal, and commons of Great Britain, in parliament assembled, had, hath, and of right ought to have, full power and authority to make laws and statutes of sufficient force and validity to bind the colonies and people of America, subjects of the crown of Great Britain, in all cases whatsoever." Moreover, Parliament concluded: "all resolutions, votes, orders, and proceedings, in any of the said colonies or plantations, whereby the power and authority of the parliament of Great Britain to make laws and the statutes as aforesaid, is denied, or drawn into question, are, and are hereby declared to be, utterly null and void to all intents and purposes whatsoever."

Failure by Americans to challenge earlier British pronouncements that the locus of imperial authority was in London was matched by their failure to recognize this Declaratory Act. In their enthusiasm over the simultaneous repeal of the Stamp Act, colonists continued to argue on the old terms by referring to the rights of Englishmen, but the frame of reference had changed. Consequently Americans faced a renewal of battles on many points which they thought had long since been settled, including representation, taxation, and the nature and origin of government. Efforts to employ old shibboleths availed nothing, and Americans were forced to abandon them and resort instead to the natural rights of man rather than those peculiar to Englishmen. This was finally and fully accomplished by the Declaration of Independence in 1776, a document which essentially repudiated concepts that had been developed and elaborated upon for three-quarters of a century.

NOTES

Introduction

1. Thomas C. Barrow, ed., "A Project for Imperial Reform: 'Hints Respecting the Settlement for Our American Provinces,' 1763," *William and Mary Quarterly*, 3d ser., XXIV (January 1967), 117.
2. (New York, 1953), esp. chaps. 6–11. This approach was dismissed forty years earlier by the dean of colonial historians: "There is nothing to show that the somewhat precise and finely spun reasoning of these intellectual leaders had any marked influence on the popular mind." Charles M. Andrews, *The Colonial Background of the American Revolution* (New Haven, 1924), p. 135.
3. (Seattle, 1965), esp. chaps. 6, 10.
4. (Chapel Hill, 1965).
5. (4 vols., Cambridge, Mass., 1965–   ), esp. chaps. 4–7. This has since been expanded and published separately as *The Ideological Origins of the American Revolution* (Cambridge, Mass., 1967).
6. *New York Times Book Review,* July 3, 1966, p. 1.
7. (3d ed., New York, 1958), pp. 6–8.
8. (New York, 1924).
9. (Cambridge, Mass., 1959).
10. (Chapel Hill, 1965).
11. (New York, 1948), p. x.

I. The Role of the Press

1. Lloyd I. Rudolph, "The Eighteenth-Century Mob in America and Europe," *American Quarterly,* XI (Winter 1959), 447–469.
2. Richard L. Merritt, "Public Opinion in Colonial America: Content-Analyzing the Colonial Press," *Public Opinion Quarterly,* XXVII (Fall 1963), 356–358, 362–365. Although imprecise, Merritt's figures suggest that by 1775 there was one issue of a newspaper for every sixty-five colonists. For the press's influence, see also Paul M. Spurlin, *Montesquieu in America, 1760–1801* (Baton Rouge, 1940), p. 42.

3. Eric L. McKitrick, *Andrew Johnson and Reconstruction* (Chicago, 1960), p. 440.

4. Leonard W. Levy, *Legacy of Suppression: Freedom of Speech and Press in Early American History* (Cambridge, Mass., 1960), p. 86.

5. More printers were attacked by legislatures than by courts or governors. *Ibid.,* pp. 20–21. But Levy's source also suggests: "And yet it would be most unfair and misleading to give the impression that the many severe and sometimes cruel dealings of the various assemblies with violators of privilege represent simply a clash of personalities with no principle behind it. If this were all, it would not be worth relating. The rights of English freemen were voiced over and over again by the various assemblies, and there is no reason to doubt the sincerity of these utterances." Mary Patterson Clark, *Parliamentary Privilege in the American Colonies* (New Haven, 1943), p. 130.

6. Carl L. Becker, *Freedom and Responsibility in the American Way of Life* (New York, 1953), pp. 2–3.

7. Some parallels can be drawn between population expansion and newspaper multiplication, though they are only tentative because of the inexactness of population statistics. Boston's first continuous paper, the *Newsletter,* began in 1704; its second, the *Gazette,* in 1719; its third, the *Courant,* in 1721. Boston's population in 1700 was 6,700; by 1722 it had increased to 10,567. Philadelphia's first paper, the *American Weekly Mercury,* started in 1719; the second, the *Gazette,* in 1728. The city's growth was rapid, with 1,200 houses in 1708 and 2,400 by 1731. New York City's first paper, the *Gazette,* began in 1725; its second, the *Weekly Journal,* in 1733, followed by the *Post Boy* in 1734. The city's population jumped from 1,460 adult males in 1723, to 2,628 males over ten in 1731, to 3,253 males over ten in 1737. For newspaper data, see Clarence Brigham, *History and Bibliography of American Newspapers 1690–1820* (2 vols., Hamden, Conn., 1962), *passim.* For the population figures, see Evarts B. Greene and Virginia D. Harrington, *American Population Before the Federal Census of 1790* (New York, 1932), pp. 22fn, 96–98, 117.

8. *New England Courant,* December 11–18, 1721 (#20).

9. Leonard W. Labaree, *et al.,* eds., *The Papers of Benjamin Franklin* (9 vols. to date, New Haven, 1959–   ), I, 27.

10. *Ibid.,* p. 47.

11. *New England Courant,* January 28–February 4, 1722/3 (#79).

12. *Ibid.,* April 20–May 6, 1723 (#92).

13. *Pennsylvania Gazette,* June 3–10, 1731 (#134). This was modified and reprinted in the *South Carolina Gazette,* October 7–14, 1732 (#89).

14. *American Weekly Mercury,* March 30–April 6, 1732 (#640).

15. Livingston Rutherfurd, *John Peter Zenger* (New York, 1904); Vincent Buranelli, *The Trial of Peter Zenger* (New York, 1957); Stanley N.

Katz, ed., *A Brief Narrative of the Case and Trial of John Peter Zenger* (Cambridge, Mass., 1964).

16. *New York Weekly Journal,* November 12, 1733 (#2), and November 19, 1733 (#3).

17. *Ibid.,* January 14, 1733/4 (#11).

18. *New York Gazette,* January 28–February 4, 1733/4 (#432).

19. *South Carolina Gazette,* February 2, 1733/4 (#1); reprinted in the *New York Weekly Journal,* March 4, 1733/4 (#18), and the *American Weekly Mercury,* March 5–12, 1733/4 (#741).

20. *Ibid.,* March 21–28, 1734 (#743), and April 18–25, 1734 (#747).

21. *New York Weekly Journal,* April 15, 1734 (#24).

22. *Ibid.,* October 21, 1734 (#51).

23. *New York Gazette,* October 21–28, 1734 (#470).

24. *New York Weekly Journal,* November 4, 1734 (#53).

25. Jonathan Blenman, *Remarks on Zengers Tryal, Taken Out of the Barbados Gazette's* (Philadelphia, 1737), pp. 3, 33–34.

26. Levy, p. 321.

27. *Pennsylvania Gazette,* November 10–17, 1737 (#466), November 17–24, 1737 (#467), November 24–December 1, 1737 (#468), December 1–8, 1737 (#469); reprinted in the *New York Weekly Journal,* December 19, 1737 (#215), December 26, 1737 (#216), January 2, 1737/8 (#217), January 17, 1737/8 (#219).

28. *American Weekly Mercury,* October 20–November 6, 1740 (#1088).

29. *American Magazine and Historical Chronicle,* I (September 1744), 556–557.

30. *Independent Advertiser,* August 8, 1748 (#32).

31. *New York Gazette, Supplement,* October 2, 1754 (#505).

32. *New York Mercury,* December 9, 1754 (#122); reprinted in the *Pennsylvania Gazette,* December 12, 1754 (#1355).

33. *New York Mercury,* January 27, 1755 (#129); reprinted in the *Virginia Gazette,* March 7, 1755 (#217).

34. *Boston Gazette or Country Journal,* April 21, 1755 (#3).

35. *Connecticut Gazette,* February 7, 1756 (#44).

36. *Boston Gazette and Country Journal,* April 26, 1756 (#56).

37. *Ibid.,* January 2, 1758 (#144).

38. Weyman's *New York Gazette,* February 22, 1762.

39. Levy, p. 18.

II. The State of Nature and the Origin of Government

1. Gordon Wood, "Rhetoric and Reality in the American Revolution," *William and Mary Quarterly,* 3d ser., XXIII (January 1966), 3–32.

2. Cotton Mather, *Lex Mercatoria: or, The Just Rules of Commerce Declared* (Boston, 1705), p. 11. Samuel Cheever, *God's Sovereign Government Among the Nations* (Boston, 1712), pp. 15–16.

3. Archibald Cummings, *The Character of a Righteous Ruler* (Philadelphia, 1736), pp. 3–4. Moses Dickinson, *A Sermon Preached Before the General Assembly of the Colony of Connecticut* (New London, 1755), pp. 7–8.

4. Thomas Maule, *Tribute to Caesar, How Paid by the Best Christians* (Philadelphia, 1712?), p. 12.

5. John Wise, *A Vindication of the Government of New England Churches* (Boston, 1717), pp. 33–38.

6. [John Webbe], *Pennsylvania Gazette,* April 8–15 and 15–22, 1736 (#384, 385). For authorship, see Leonard W. Labaree, ed., *The Papers of Benjamin Franklin* (New Haven, 1959–   ), II, 146.

7. Samuel Chew, *The Speech of Samuel Chew, Esq. Chief Justice of the Government of New Castle, Kent, and Sussex Upon Delaware* (Philadelphia, 1741), pp. 4–7.

8. Jared Eliot, *Give Caesar His Due. Or, the Obligation that Subjects Are Under to Their Civil Rulers* (New London, 1738), p. 27.

9. Elisha Williams, *The Essential Rights and Liberties of Protestants* (Boston, 1744), pp. 2–3.

10. [Boston] *Independent Advertiser,* April 10, 1749 (#67).

11. Milton M. Klein, ed., *The Independent Reflector* (Cambridge, 1963), pp. 287–288.

12. *New York Mercury,* September 10 and 17, 1753 (#57, 58).

13. "Rusticus," *The Good of the Community Impartially Considered* (Boston, 1754), pp 32–33. *Pennsylvania Journal,* September 26, 1754 (#616). *Ibid.,* May 11, 1758 (#805); reprinted in *New York Mercury,* May 22, 1758 (#301). Abraham Williams, *A Sermon Preached at Boston Before the Great and General Court or Assembly . . .* (Boston, 1762), pp. 3–11.

14. Samuel Willard, *The Character of a Good Ruler* (Boston, 1694), pp. 2–3, 7, 9, 13, 15–18, 20–21.

15. Ebenezer Pemberton, *The Divine Original of Government Asserted* (Boston, 1710), p. 85.

16. Maule, *Tribute to Caesar,* p. 12. John Woodward, *Civil Rulers Are God's Ministers, For the People's Good* (Boston, 1712), pp. 3–4. Samuel Cheever, *God's Sovereign Government,* pp. 14–16.

17. Joseph Moss, *An Election Sermon Preached Before the General Assembly of the Colony of Connecticut . . .* (New London, 1715), pp. 6–7.

18. John Wise, *A Vindication,* pp. 44–46.

19. *American Weekly Mercury,* March 16–23, 1721 (#66).

20. William Burnham, *God's Providence in Placing Men in Their Respective Stations and Conditions Asserted and Shewed* (New London, 1722), p. 40.

21. *New England Courant,* May 21–28, 1722 (#43).

22. *Ibid.,* June 22–29, 1724 (#152).

23. *The Universal Instructor in All Arts and Sciences: and the Pennsylvania Gazette,* April 3, 1729 (#15). *New York Weekly Journal,* November 26, 1733 (#4).

24. Jeremiah Wise, *Rulers the Ministers of God for the Good of Their People* (Boston, 1729), pp. 18–19. Nathaniel Chauncey, *The Faithful Ruler Described and Excited* (New London, 1734), pp. 1–3.

25. John Barnard, *The Throne Established by Righteousness* (Boston, 1734), pp. 7–8, 12–17.

26. Eliot, *Give Caesar His Due,* pp. 31–32.

27. Chew, *Speech,* p. 5. *American Weekly Mercury,* June 24–July 1, 1742 (#1174). Samuel Chew, *The Speech of . . .* (Philadelphia, 1742), p. 2.

28. [Elisha Williams], *The Essential Rights and Liberties of Protestants* (Boston, 1744), pp. 4–5.

29. James Allen, *Magistracy an Institution of Christ Upon the Throne* (Boston, 1744), pp. 22–27, 40.

30. Samuel Hall, *The Legislatures Right, Charge, and Duty in Respect of Religion* (New London, 1746), pp. 1, 12–13.

31. *New York Evening Post,* August 3, 1747 (#141).

32. *Ibid.,* December 7, 1747 (#157). Reprinted in *Boston Evening Post,* December 28, 1747 (#646).

33. [Boston] *Independent Advertiser,* January 11, 1748 (#2); February 29, 1748 (#9). *Pennsylvania Gazette,* May 27, 1750 (#1431).

34. Samuel Philips, *Political Rulers Authorized and Influenc'd By God Our Saviour, To Decree and Execute Justice* (Boston, 1750), pp. 6, 33.

35. Noah Hobart, *Civil Government The Foundation of Social Happiness* (New London, 1751), pp. 1–3.

36. William Welsteed, *The Dignity and Duty of the Civil Magistrate* (Boston, 1751), pp. 6–9, 11–12.

37. *Boston Weekly Newsletter,* May 9, 1751 (#2555). *Independent Reflector,* July 12, 1753 (#33).

38. *New York Mercury,* September 17, 1753 (#58).

39. "Rusticus," *The Good of the Community,* p. 32. Jonathan Mayhew, *A Sermon Preached in the Audience of His Excellency William Shirley* (Boston, 1754), pp. 3–7, 10, 20.

40. Daniel Fowle, *An Appendix to the Late Total Eclipse of Liberty* (Boston, 1756), pp. 3–5.

41. Moses Dickinson, *A Sermon,* pp. 6–8, 10.

42. Thomas Frink, *A King Reigning in Righteousness, and Princes Ruling in Judgment* (Boston, 1758), pp. 71–72.

43. James Lockwood, *The Worth and Excellence of Civil Freedom and Liberty Illustrated, and a Public Spirit and The Love of Our Country Recommended* (New London, 1759), p. 10.

44. Benjamin Stevens, *A Sermon Preached at Boston* . . . (Boston, 1761), pp. 8–9.

45. Abraham Williams, *A Sermon Preached at Boston* . . . (Boston, 1762), p. 8.

46. James Otis, *A Vindication of the Conduct of the House of Representatives of the Province of the Massachusetts–Bay* . . . (Boston, 1762), pp. 17–20.

III. Religion and the State

1. Thomas Maule, *Tribute to Caesar, How Paid by the Best Christians* (Philadelphia, 1712), p. 12.

2. Josiah Smith, *Humane Impositions Proved Unscriptural, Or, The Divine Right of Private Judgment* (Boston, 1729), p. 10.

3. *American Weekly Mercury*, June 18–25, 1730 (#547).

4. See Wesley F. Craven, *The Legend of the Founding Fathers* (New York, 1956), pp. 20–33.

5. *Boston Weekly News Letter*, December 2–9, 1731 (#1454).

6. *Rhode Island Gazette*, January 11, 1733 (#15).

7. *Pennsylvania Gazette*, May 6–13, 1736 (#388).

8. *Ibid.*, March 21–28, 1737/8 (#485).

9. John Barnard, *The Lord Jesus Christ the Only, and Supreme Head of the Church* (Boston, 1738), pp. 26–27.

10. Peter Clark, *The Rulers Highest Dignity, and the People's Truest Glory* (Boston, 1739), pp. 18–19.

11. John Callendar, *An Historical Discourse on the Civil and Religious Affairs of the Colony of Rhode-Island and Providence Plantations in New England in America* (Boston, 1739), pp. 14–16.

12. Charles Chauncy, *The Only Compulsion Proper to Be Made Use of in the Affairs of Conscience and Religion* (Boston, 1739), p. 9.

13. William Cooper, *The Honours of Christ Demanded of the Magistrate* (Boston, 1740), pp. 13, 22.

14. *American Weekly Mercury*, January 15–22, 1739/40 (#1047).

15. Samuel Chew, *The Speech of* . . . (Philadelphia, 1742), pp. 2–3.

16. *American Weekly Mercury*, March 15–22, 1743/4 (#1263); *Pennsylvania Journal or Weekly Advertiser*, March 21, 1743/4 (#69)—both reprinted from the *American Magazine*, January 1743/4.

17. *New York Weekly Post Boy, Postscript*, May 21, 1744 (#70).

18. *Pennsylvania Journal or Weekly Advertiser,* January 5, 1747/8 (#268); reprinted in the *Pennsylvania Gazette,* January 19, 1747/8 (#997).

19. Jonathan Mayhew, *Seven Sermons Upon the Following Subjects* (Boston, 1749), pp. 57–58, 82–84.

20. Anon., *A Letter to a Gentleman, Containing a Plea for the Rights of Conscience, in Things of a Religious Nature* (Boston, 1753), p. 3.

21. *New York Gazette Revived in the Weekly Post Boy,* February 12, 1753 (#524).

22. *New York Mercury,* July 23, 1753 (#50).

23. *Ibid.,* July 30, 1753 (#51).

24. *Independent Reflector,* August 2, 1753 (#36).

25. *New York Mercury,* August 27, 1753 (#55), September 17, 1753 (#58).

26. *Independent Reflector,* September 27, 1753 (#44).

27. *Occasional Reverberator,* October 5, 1753 (#4).

28. *New York Mercury,* March 24, 1755 (#137).

29. Moses Dickinson, *A Sermon Preached Before the General Assembly of the Colony of Connecticut* (New London, 1755), pp. 23–24, 27, 29–30.

30. *Connecticut Gazette,* October 15, 1757 (#132).

31. William Hart, *A Letter to Paulinus; Containing an Answer to His Three Questions, Lately Proposed to the Public, in the Connecticut Gazette* (New Haven, 1760), pp. 5–6.

32. John Bolles, *To Worship God in Spirit, and in Truth, Is to Worship Him in the True Liberty of Conscience* (Boston, 1756), pp. 60–61.

33. Benjamin Stevens, *A Sermon Preached at Boston* (Boston, 1761), pp. 10–11.

34. Abraham Williams, *A Sermon Preached at Boston, Before the Great and General Court or Assembly* (Boston, 1762), pp. 10–11.

IV. Constitutional Theory and the British Constitution

1. R. M. MacIver, "European Doctrines and the Constitution," in Conyers Read, ed., *The Constitution Reconsidered* (New York, 1938), p. 51. Alice M. Baldwin, *The New England Clergy and the American Revolution* (Durham, N.C., 1928), p. 88.

2. Samuel Willard, *The Character of a Good Ruler* (Boston, 1694), p. 18.

3. Ebenezer Pemberton, *The Divine Original Dignity of Government Asserted* (Boston, 1710), pp. 12, 86.

4. Joseph Moss, *An Election Sermon Preached Before the General Assembly of the Colony of Connecticut* (New London, 1715), pp. 6–7.

5. *American Weekly Mercury,* September 20–27, 1733 (#717).

6. *Pennsylvania Gazette,* April 8–15, 1736 (#384).

7. Baldwin, p. 88.

8. James Allen, *Magistracy an Institution of Christ Upon the Throne* (Boston, 1744), p. 26. Charles Chauncy, *Civil Magistrates Must Be Just, Ruling in Fear of God* (Boston, 1747), pp. 14–16.

9. *New York Evening Post,* December 7, 1747 (#157); reprinted in *Boston Evening Post,* December 28, 1747 (#646).

10. *Independent Reflector,* December 21, 1752 (#4), p. 13.

11. *Ibid.,* July 12, 1753 (#33), p. 133; August 16, 1753 (#38), p. 151.

12. William Douglass, *A Summary, Historical and Political, of the First Planting, Progressive Improvements, and Present State of the British Settlements in North America* (2 vols., Boston, 1749), I, 214. "The Watchman, Letter VII," *Pennsylvania Journal and Weekly Advertiser,* August 17, 1758 (#819).

13. *A Letter to the People of Pennsylvania; Occasioned by the Assembly's Passing That Important Act, for Constituting the Judges of the Supreme Courts and Common Pleas During Good Behaviour* (Philadelphia, 1760), pp. 3–5.

14. James Logan, *The Charge Delivered from the Bench to the Grand Jury* (Philadelphia, 1723), pp. 4–5.

15. Pennsylvania Assembly, *To the Honourable Patrick Gordon, Esq.: Lieut. Governour* (Philadelphia, 1728), p. 6.

16. *Boston Gazette,* July 22–29, 1728 (#453).

17. [Boston] *Weekly Newsletter,* July 18–25, 1728 (#82); *New England Weekly Journal,* July 29, 1728 (#71); *New York Gazette,* July 29–August 5, 1728 (#144). Burnet's statement was quoted verbatim by Governor William Shirley in a similar dispute. *Pennsylvania Gazette,* March 3, 1741/2 (#690).

18. *New York Gazette,* March 4, 1733/4 (#436).

19. *Ibid.,* March 11–18, 1733/4 (#438).

20. *Ibid.,* October 21–28, 1734 (#470).

21. *Ibid.,* October 27–November 3, 1735 (#523).

22. *Pennsylvania Gazette,* April 1–8, 1736 (#383).

23. *Ibid.,* April 8–15, 1736 (#384).

24. *American Weekly Mercury,* June 10–17, 1736 (#859).

25. *Pennsylvania Gazette,* March 21–28, 1737 (#485). Reprinted in the *American Magazine, or, A Monthly Review of the Political State of the British Colonies,* I (January 1740/1), 26.

26. [Boston] *Independent Advertiser,* January 11, 1748 (#2).

27. *Maryland Gazette,* February 10, 1748 (#146).

28. *Ibid.,* March 16, 1748 (#151).

29. *Ibid.,* April 27, 1748 (#157).

30. *Ibid.,* May 11, 1748 (#159).

31. *The Maryland Gazette Extraordinary: An Appendix* (to #162), June 4, 1748.
32. [Boston] *Independent Advertiser,* February 6, 1749 (#58); *Boston Post-Boy,* October 9, 1752 (#927); William Welsteed, *The Dignity and Duty of the Civil Magistrate* (Boston, 1751), p. 33.
33. Anon., *Some Observations on the Bill* (Boston, 1754), p. 2. See also *Pennsylvania Gazette,* June 30, 1757 (#1488), for a discussion of an "anticonstitutional" bill.
34. *Boston Gazette and Country Journal,* May 10, 1756 (#58).
35. Anon., *A Letter to a Friend Occasioned by the Unhappy Controversy at Wallingford* (New Haven, 1760), p. 5 fn. See pp. 84–85 above.
36. *New York Gazette, or Weekly Post-Boy,* November 1, 1756 (#720).

v. The Colonial Constitutions

1. *Journal of the Votes and Proceedings of the General Assembly of the Colony of New York* (2 vols., New York, 1764–1766), I, 306–307.
2. William Smith, *Mr. Smith's Opinion Humbly Offered to the General Assembly of the Colony of New York, on the Seventh of June, 1734 at Their Request* (New York, 1734), pp. 12–13, 33–34.
3. Joseph Murray, *Mr. Murray's Opinion Relating to the Courts of Justice in the Colony of New York; Delivered to the General Assembly of the Said Colony, At Their Request, the 12th of June, 1734* (New York, 1734), pp. 2, 15.
4. *American Weekly Mercury,* April 5–12, 1739 (#1005); reprinted in *Pennsylvania Gazette,* April 12–19, 1739 (#540).
5. George Clarke, *The Speech of the Honourable George Clarke, Esq.* (New York, 1739), n.p.; reprinted in *New York Gazette,* October 1–8, 1739 (#725).
6. *American Weekly Mercury,* April 24–May 1, 1740 (#1061).
7. Anon., *Extracts from the Minutes and Votes of the House of Assembly of the Colony of New Jersey . . . To Which Are Added Some Notes and Observations upon the Said Votes* (Philadelphia, 1743), pp. 7–8.
8. *New York Weekly Post Boy,* December 23, 1745 (#153).
9. *N.Y. Assembly Journal,* II, 125.
10. George Clinton, *A Message from His Excellency the Honourable George Clinton . . . To the General Assembly . . . The Thirteenth of October 1747* (New York, 1747), p. 2.
11. *N.Y. Assembly Journal,* II, 211.
12. *Boston Evening Post,* December 28, 1747 (#646); reprinted from *New York Evening Post,* December 7, 1747 (#157).
13. *New York Gazette Revived in the Weekly Post Boy,* January 18, 1747/8 (#261).

14. *Pennsylvania Gazette*, August 10, 1749 (#1078).

15. *New York Gazette Revived in the Weekly Post Boy*, September 10, 1750 (#399).

16. *Pennsylvania Journal and Weekly Advertiser*, July 4, 1754 (#604); reprinted in *Boston Gazette, or Weekly Advertiser*, July 30, 1754 (#83), and August 6, 1754 (#84).

17. [New York] *American Chronicle*, April 12, 1761 (I, #4).

18. Maryland Assembly, *The Charter of Maryland, Together with the Debates and Proceedings of the Upper and Lower Houses of Assembly, in the Years 1722, 1723, and 1724* (Philadelphia, 1725), pp. 2–3, 12, 19–20.

19. Anon., *A Letter from a Gentleman in Philadelphia to His Friend in Bucks.* (Philadelphia, 1728), p. 2. See also, Anon., *The Proceedings of Some Members of Assembly, at Philadelphia, April 1728, Vindicated from the Unfair Reasoning and Unjust Insinuations of a Certain Remarker* (Philadelphia, 1728), pp. 1–2.

20. Anon., *Proceedings of Some Members of Assembly, at Philadelphia, April 1728,* p. 1. *American Weekly Mercury,* December 18–24, 1728 (#468).

21. *Pennsylvania Gazette,* March 21–28, 1737/8 (#485).

22. *American Magazine, Or, A Monthly Review of the Political State of the British Colonies,* I (January 1740/1), 17–29.

23. *Pennsylvania Gazette,* October 2, 1755 (#1397).

24. *Pennsylvania Journal and Weekly Advertiser: Supplement,* March 25, 1756 (#694); reprinted in *New York Mercury,* April 5, 1756 (#191), and *New York Gazette or The Weekly Post Boy,* April 5, 1756 (#690).

25. *Pennsylvania Gazette,* November 24, 1757 (#1509).

26. *American Magazine, and Monthly Chronicle,* I (February 1758), 210–224. Also in *Pennsylvania Gazette,* January 19, 1758 (#1517), and January 26, 1758 (#1518).

27. *New York Mercury: Supplement,* September 18, 1758 (#318).

28. Maryland Province, *A Bill for Raising a Supply for His Majesty's Service* (Annapolis, 1762), pp. 4–5, 9.

29. *New England Weekly Journal,* March 18, 1728 (#52).

30. *New York Gazette,* August 12–19, 1728 (#146), and August 19–26, 1728 (#147); reprinted in [Boston] *Weekly News Letter,* September 5–12, 1728 (#89), and September 12–19, 1728 (#90); also *New England Weekly Journal,* September 9, 1728 (#77).

31. Anon., *Question: Are We Obliged in This Government of the Massachusetts, By Charter, To Settle a Salary Upon the Governor?* (Boston, 1729), pp. 1–2.

32. *Pennsylvania Gazette,* September 25, 1729 (#39); reprinted from *New England Weekly Journal,* September 8, 1729 (#129); see also *New York Gazette,* September 15–22, 1729 (#203).

33. [Boston] *Weekly News Letter,* September 11–18, 1729 (#142).

34. *Extract from the Political State of Great Britain for the Month of December, 1730* (Boston, 1731), p. 14.

35. *Boston Weekly News Letter,* January 20–27, 1732 (#1461). See also *Boston Gazette,* January 24–31, 1732 (#631); [Boston] *Weekly Rehearsal,* January 31, 1732 (#19), and *New England Weekly Journal,* January 31, 1732 (#254).

36. *Rhode Island Gazette,* January 11, 1735 (#15).

37. Americanus, *A Letter to the Freeholders and Other Inhabitants of the Massachusetts Bay Relating to Their Approaching Election of Representatives* (Newport, R.I., 1739), pp. 2–4.

38. *New England Weekly Journal,* January 13, 1741 (#717). See also *Boston Weekly News Letter,* January 8–15, 1741 (#1921), and *Boston Weekly Post-Boy,* January 12, 1741 (#353).

39. Jeremiah Dummer, *A Defense of the New England Charters* (Boston, 1721), p. 5. In the 1745 Boston edition, see p. 4.

40. [Boston] *Independent Advertiser,* November 21, 1748 (#47).

41. *Ibid.,* January 23, 1749 (#56).

42. *Boston Gazette and Country Journal,* May 10, 1756 (#58).

43. *Boston Evening Post,* April 27, 1761 (#1339).

VI. Rights and Liberties

1. Jefferson to Henry Lee, May 8, 1825, in Adrienne Koch and William Peden, eds., *The Life and Selected Writings of Thomas Jefferson* (New York, 1944), p. 719.

2. *Boston Weekly Post-Boy,* February 2, 1741 (#357).

3. As an example, see Leonard W. Levy and Lawrence H. Leder, " 'Exotic Fruit': The Right Against Compulsory Self-Incrimination in Colonial New York," *William and Mary Quarterly,* 3d ser., XX (January 1963), 3–32.

4. Jeremiah Dummer, *A Defence of the New England Charters* (Boston, 1721), p. 10. *The New-England Courant,* July 23–30, 1732 (#52).

5. [Isaac Norris], *The Speech Delivered from the Bench in the Court of Common Pleas . . . Philadelphia, the 11th Day of September, 1727* (Philadelphia, 1727), p. 2.

6. *Boston Gazette,* September 1–8, 1729 (#511).

7. *American Weekly Mercury,* August 2–9, 1733 (#710); reprinted in *New York Weekly Journal,* December 3, 1733 (#5).

8. William Smith, *Mr. Smith's Opinion Humbly Offered to the General Assembly of the Colony of New York, on the Seventh of June, 1734 at Their Request* (New York, 1734), pp. 12–13, 34.

9. Joseph Murray, *Mr. Murray's Opinion Relating to the Courts of Justice in the Colony of New York* (New York, 1734), p. 2.

10. John Wright, *The Speech of John Wright, Esq., One of the Magistrates of Lancaster County* (Philadelphia, 1741), p. 2; reprinted in *Boston Weekly Post-Boy,* June 29, 1741 (#378).

11. *New York Mercury,* July 28, 1755 (#155).

12. *Pennsylvania Journal and Weekly Advertiser,* February 2, 1758 (#791).

13. *Ibid.,* February 23, 1758 (#794).

14. *Boston Evening Post,* April 27, 1761 (#1339).

15. *American Magazine and Monthly Chronicle for the British Colonies,* I (February 1758), p. 210.

16. *Journal of the Votes and Proceedings of the General Assembly of the Colony of New York* (2 vols., New York, 1764–1766), I, 223–224.

17. Samuel Mulford, *Samuel Mulford's Speech to the Assembly at New York, April the Second, 1714* (New York, 1714), p. 6.

18. Anon., *A Collection of the Proceedings of the Great and General Court or Assembly . . . of the Massachusetts Bay* (Boston, 1729), p. 12.

19. *Maryland Gazette,* January 20, 1748 (#143); February 10, 1748 (#146); March 16, 1748 (#151); March 23, 1748 (Supplement to #152); April 20, 1748 (#156); April 27, 1748 (#157); May 4, 1748 (#158); May 11, 1748 (#159); June 4, 1748 (Appendix to #162).

20. *Independent Reflector,* December 7, 1752 (#2). *Pennsylvania Gazette,* April 20, 1758 (#1530); reprinted in *New American Magazine,* April 1758 (#4).

21. *New York Mercury,* May 22, 1758 (#301); reprinted from *Pennsylvania Journal,* May 11, 1758 (#805).

22. *New York Weekly Journal,* June 16, 1735 (#84).

23. Anon., *The Charter of Maryland, Together with the Debates and Proceedings of the Upper and Lower Houses of Assembly . . . 1722, 1723, and 1724* (Philadelphia, 1725), pp. iii, iv, 12, 20.

24. Pennsylvania Assembly, *To the Honourable Patrick Gordon, Esq.: Lieut. Governor* (Philadelphia, 1728), p. 5.

25. [Boston] *Weekly Rehearsal,* January 24, 1732 (#18).

26. Samuel Chew, *Speech* (Philadelphia, 1741), pp. 4–5.

27. [Elisha Williams], *The Essential Rights and Liberties of Protestants* (Boston, 1744), pp. 2–6.

28. *New York Evening Post,* May 25, 1747 (#131).

29. *Boston Evening Post,* December 28, 1747 (#646); reprinted from *New York Evening Post,* December 7, 1747 (#157). [Boston] *Independent Advertiser,* June 13, 1748.

30. *New York Gazette Revived in the Weekly Post Boy,* January 9, 1748/9 (#312).

31. *Pennsylvania Gazette,* November 21, 1754 (#1352). *New York Gazette Revived in the Weekly Post Boy,* April 16, 1753 (#533).

32. [New Haven] *Connecticut Gazette,* April 10, 1756 (#53). *Boston Gazette and Country Journal,* May 10, 1756 (#58).

33. Edward Mead Earle, ed., *The Federalist* (New York, c. 1937), p. 559 (Modern Library edition).

VII. The Concept of Empire: A Fatal Flaw

1. John Palmer, *The Present State of New England Impartially Considered, In a Letter to the Clergy* (Boston, 1689), pp. 10–11.

2. Anon., *Revolution in New England Justified, and the People There Vindicated From the Aspersions Cast Upon them by Mr. John Palmer, In His Pretended Answer to the Declaration, Published by the Inhabitants of Boston* (Boston, 1691), pp. 6–8, 42–43.

3. Francis Makemie, *A Narrative of a New and Unusual American Imprisonment of Two Presbyterian Ministers and Prosecution of Mr. Francis Makemie* (New York, 1707), pp. 4–5, 18–19, 22.

4. William Bradford, *The Humble Representation of the General Assembly of Her Majesty's Province of New Jersey to His Excellency Robert Hunter* (New York, 1710), p. 5. See also, Samuel Jennings, *The Reply of the House of Representatives of the Province of New Jersey, to an Answer Made by His Excellency Edward Viscount Cornbury* (New York, 1707), pp. 8–10.

5. *American Weekly Mercury,* January 31–February 7, 1721 (#60); reprinted in *Boston News Letter,* January 2–9, 1721 (#878).

6. Lewis Morris, *Some Observations on the Charge Given by the Honourable James DeLancey, Esq.; Chief Justice of the Province of New York, to the Grand Jury, the 15th Day of January, 1733* (New York, 1733/4), pp. 9–10.

7. *American Weekly Mercury,* December 30–January 6, 1735/6 (#836).

8. *New York Weekly Post Boy,* April 29, 1745 (#119).

9. *Journal of the Votes and Proceedings of the General Assembly of the Colony of New York* (2 vols., New York, 1764–1766), II, 258.

10. William Douglass, *A Summary, Historical and Political, of the First Planting, Progressive Improvements, and Present State of the British Settlements in North America* (Boston, 1749), I, 205–207, 212.

11. *New York Gazette Revived in the Weekly Post Boy,* January 27, 1752 (#471).

12. *New York Mercury,* February 17, 1755 (p. 132), and *Supplement.*

13. Archibald Kennedy, *A Speech Said to Have Been Delivered Some Time Before the Close of the Last Sessions, by a Member Dissenting from the Church* (New York, 1755), pp. 6–8.

14. *Journal of the Votes and Proceedings of the General Assembly of the Colony of New York* (2 vols., New York, 1764–1766), II, 673.
15. [New York] *American Chronicle,* I (April 19, 1762), #5.
16. [James Otis?], *Boston Gazette and Country Journal,* January 4, 1762 (#353).
17. See the various legal opinions collected in George Chalmers, ed., *Opinions of Eminent Lawyers on Various Points of English Jurisprudence* (Burlington, N.J., 1858), pp. 206, 208, 239, 256, 265–266, 376, 377, 439–440, 511.

VIII. The Ideological Discontinuity

1. J. Huizinga, *The Waning of the Middle Ages* (New York, 1954); see especially the preface. Carl L. Becker, *The Heavenly City of the Eighteenth-Century Philosophers* (New Haven, 1932), pp. 28–31.
2. John P. Roche, ed., *Origins of American Political Thought* (New York, 1967), pp. 11–13, 18.
3. John C. Miller, *Origins of the American Revolution* (Boston, 1943), pp. 288–292.
4. See above, p. 60.

BIBLIOGRAPHICAL NOTE

THE SOURCES for this book, as I have mentioned on several occasions in the text, are the varied emanations of the American presses from the years 1689 to 1763. Rather than attempt to list each book and run of a newspaper that has been examined, I have thought it best to indicate where these materials may be consulted, allowing the references within the text to carry the rest of the burden.

For colonial newspapers, the indispensable guide is Clarence S. Brigham, *History and Bibliography of American Newspapers, 1690–1820* (2 vols., Worcester, Mass., 1947). A good many of the newspapers listed by Brigham are now available in a microcard edition published under the auspices and with the cooperation of the American Antiquarian Society, the depository of the most complete collection of these materials. Many other runs of newspapers, which have been collated with the holdings of other libraries and which contain all known copies, have been microfilmed by several depositories. The Institute of Early American History and Culture at Williamsburg, Virginia, has the most complete file of these, and it has available a mimeographed descriptive list of its holdings. The University of Washington Library in Seattle has a microfilm of the [Boston] *Independent Advertiser* from 1748 through 1749 (the file of the original copies is in the Boston Public Library), and the *Connecticut Gazette*, 1755–1768, taken from the originals at the Yale University Library. The New York Historical Society owns the most complete files of three papers: Weyman's *New York Gazette,* the *New York Evening Post,* and the *New York Gazette or Weekly Post Boy.*

Colonial magazines are fully described in Frank Luther Mott's *A History of American Magazines* (3 vols., New York, 1930–1938).

These have been collated and collected by University Microfilms and published as a set in microfilm under the series title "American Periodicals, Eighteenth Century." The colonial periodicals provide a valuable and little-used source for all phases of early American history. The difficulty in using them stems from the lack of an overall index and the need to review the contents of all thirty-three microfilm rolls.

For all other printed materials the standard guide is Charles Evans, *American Bibliography: A Chronological Dictionary of Books, Pamphlets, and Periodical Literature Printed in the United States . . . 1639 . . . 1820* (12 vols., Chicago, 1903–1934). Listing all materials printed up to 1800 (despite the date given in the title), it is invaluable. Based upon its listing and numerical designation of items, a microcard edition of all the works has been published. It is complete except for periodicals, fugitive pieces that Evans reported on the basis of hearsay evidence, and a few items that have since disappeared. Through the year 1762 there are approximately 9,200 items in this collection.

Almost all of the research for this study has been done by means of microfilm and microcard collections. The three major sources listed above, by bringing together and making readily available the resources of the greatest libraries in America and abroad, have revolutionized at least some aspects of scholarly research.

INDEX

"A Freeholder," 90–91, 100, 123
"A Truman," 135
Act of Union, 93
Adams, Randolph G., 13
Admiralty courts, 12
Alexander, James, 28–29
Allen, James, 52–53, 82
American Magazine, 67–68
American Magazine and Historical Chronicle, 30–31
American Revolution, 13–14
American Weekly Mercury: on liberty of conscience, 62, 63; on power of parliament, 89; on press freedom, 24–25, 26
"Americano-Britannus," 92, 124
"Americanus," 113
Andros, Sir Edmund, 132–133, 138–139
Anglican Church. *See* Church of England.
"Anti-Z," 89
"Aristotimus," 72–73
Aristotle, 84
Authoritarianism, 48–49

Bailyn, Bernard, 14
Baldwin, Alice M., 80, 82
Baptists, 74
Barbados, 28
Barnard, John, 51–52, 64–65
Bastille, 19
Becker, Carl, 22, 140
Belcher, Jonathan, 63, 101, 112–114
Bill of Rights, 130
Bland, Richard, 12

Bolles, John, 76
Boorstin, Daniel, 16
Boston Evening Post, 116, 121–122
Boston Gazette, 34, 35, 93
Boston Gazette and Country Journal, 129
(Boston) *Independent Advertiser,* 31, 43–44, 54, 90
Boston Weekly Newsletter, 57
Boston Weekly Post Boy, 118
(Boston) *Weekly Rehearsal,* 126
Bracton, Henry De, 88
Bradford, Andrew, 24, 25, 30
Bradford, William, 25, 27
Brigham, Clarence S., 161
Burleigh, Henry T., 89
Burnet, William, 87, 109–112, 119, 123
Burnham, William, 49

Callendar, John, 65–66
Care, Henry, 125
"Cato, Junior," 81–82
Cato Letters, 25
Charles I, 101
Charles II, 103, 133
Charleston, S.C., 25
Chauncey, Nathaniel, 51
Chauncy, Charles, 66, 82–83
Cheever, Samuel, 39, 47
Chew, Samuel, 42, 52, 67, 68
Children, status of, 42–43
Church of England: in England, 73; and King's College, 70–71, 137–138; in Massachusetts, 69; and Presbyterians, 74, 134
Church of Scotland, 73

Civil War, 37
Clarendon, Earl of. *See*
    Hyde, Edward.
Clark, Peter, 65
Clarke, George, 97–98
Clinton, George, 99, 100–101, 136
Coke, Sir Edward, 119
Colbourn, Trevor, 14, 16
Colden, Cadwallader, 138
Connecticut, 74–76
Connecticut Gazette, 34–35, 75,
    129
Conscience, liberty of. *See* Liberty
    of conscience.
Constitution, English, 12, 135, 137
Constitutionalism, concept of, 12,
    31–32, 93
Cooper, William, 66
Cornbury. *See* Hyde, Edward.
Cosby, William, 29
Cotton, John, 76
Cummings, Archibald, 39

Declaration of Independence, 118,
    140, 146
Declaratory Act, 145
Denny, William, 107–108, 124
Dependency, theories of, 132–133
Dickinson, Moses, 39, 59, 74–75
Douglass, William, 84, 136
Dummer, Jeremiah, 114, 119

Editorial opinion, 20–21
Eliot, Jared, 42, 52
Evans, Charles, 163

Federalist Papers, 130
Feudalism, 19
Fowle, Daniel, 58–59
France, 70
Franklin, Benjamin, 12, 23–24,
    119
Franklin, James, 22–23, 119
Freeborn, William, 63, 113
Freedom, understanding of, 22
French and Indian War, 11
Frink, Thomas, 59

Glorious Revolution, 11, 37, 80, 88,
    89, 101
Goals, American, 20
Gordon, Patrick, 39, 87, 103, 126
Gordon Riots, 19
Gordon, Thomas, 25
Great Awakening, 74
Greece, 87

Hall, Samuel, 52
Hamilton, Alexander, 130
Hamilton, Andrew, 28, 30
Hart, William, 75–76
Hobart, Noah, 52
Hobbes, Thomas, 37, 38–40, 41, 42
Hooker, Thomas, 12
Hopkinson, Francis, 128
Huizinga, Johan, 140
Hunter, Robert, 122–123
Hyde, Edward, 74, 133–134

Ideology, importance of, 14
Impeachment, 107, 112
Independent Reflector: on limits of
    power, 83; on locus of power, 57;
    on religious dispute, 71; on state
    of nature, 44
Institute of Early American History
    and Culture, 161
Ireland, 136

Jefferson, Thomas, 12, 118
Jensen, Merrill, 13–14
Jones, Sir William, 133
Judiciary: as balance in govern-
    ment, 85; limited by Act of
    Union, 93; role in English
    liberties, 122; role in New Jersey,
    101
Jury trials, 118, 120–121, 125

Keith, Sir William, 50
Kennedy, Archibald, 138
King George's War, 68
King's College, 70–71, 74, 137

"Layman," 53
Legislative privilege, 21
Legislative rights, 14

Levy, Leonard, 36
Libel. *See* Seditious libel.
Liberty: attitude toward 11, 19;
    definitions of, 20, 121, 123,
    125–126, 129, 133; and Glorious
    Revolution, 88; imprecision of,
    126, 129–130, 144; and licen-
    tiousness, 26; and Magna Carta,
    129; nature of, 127–128,
    144–145; and power, 127;
    preservation of, 127–128; and
    property, 125
Liberty of conscience: in Connecti-
    cut, 75; in Massachusetts, 65–66,
    76–77; meaning of, 77–78; in
    Pennsylvania, 68–69
Licentiousness, 30, 32
Literacy, 15, 20
Livingston, William: on common
    law in colonies, 137; on govern-
    ment and religion, 71–73; on
    power, 57, 83–84; on state of
    nature, 44–45; on taxation, 124
Locke, John, 81; appeal of, 38;
    criticized, 42–43; ideas of,
    adapted, 40, 82, 105; on state of
    nature, 37, 38, 42, 142
Lockwood, James, 59
Logan, James, 86
London Journal, 23
Loyalty, 31

MacIver, R. M., 79–80
Magna Carta: applicability to
    colonies, 97, 120, 132, 137; fixed
    and static, 93; importance of to
    colonists, 111, 119; meaning
    of, 91, 119, 121, 129
Majority rule, 126
Makemie, Francis, 74, 133–134
Maryland: assembly claims power,
    102, 108; assembly disputes
    council, 104, 108; conquered
    province theory, 102; constitu-
    tion of, 102, 104–105, 125–126;
    council's power, 104–105, 108;
    tax controversy, 108
Maryland Gazette, 90

Massachusetts: assembly censors
    press, 23; assembly disputes
    governor's salary, 109–114;
    assembly's role, 45, 63, 87, 116;
    assembly's similarity to parlia-
    ment, 110, 112–113; assembly's
    tax power, 112–113, 123; claims
    Magna Carta, 111, 119; constitu-
    tion of, 113, 114–115; denies
    parallel with other colonies,
    110–112; religion in, 63, 64–65,
    69, 76
Mather, Cotton, 38–39
Maule, Thomas, 40, 41, 47,
    61–62, 77
Mayflower Compact, 140
Mayhew, Jonathan, 12, 58, 69–70
McKitrick, Eric L., 20
Mobs and liberty, 19
Moore, William, 107, 108, 122
Morris, Lewis, 28, 97, 98, 135–136
Morris, Robert Hunter, 105
Moss, Joseph, 47, 81
Mott, Frank Luther, 162
Mulford, Samuel, 122–123
Murray, Joseph, 96–97, 120

"Native of Maryland," 91–92
New England, Dominion of,
    132–133, 138–139
New England, religion in, 62–63
New England Courant, 22, 23, 49
New England Weekly Journal, 109
New Jersey: assembly's power,
    136; constitution of, 97, 101;
    difficulties in, 98, 101, 134;
    relationship to England, 135–136
New Lights, 74
New York: assembly on liberty
    and power, 127; assembly on
    taxation, 122; Church of
    England in, 74; and empire, 136,
    138; on governmental power, 83,
    96; and Governor Clinton,
    99–101; and King's College
    controversy, 70–71, 74
New York City, 24–25, 88
New York Gazette, 25, 27, 32

New York Gazette (Weyman's),
    35–36
New York Historical Society, 161
New York Mercury, 32–34, 44–45,
    73
New York Weekly Journal, 25, 27
New York Weekly Post Boy, 68
Nicholls, William, 134
Norris, Isaac, 119

Occasional Reverberator, 73
Osgood, Herbert Levi, 15
Otis, James, 60, 142–143

Paine, Thomas, 19, 52
Palmer, John, 132, 133
Parental rule, 42, 43
Parker, James, 32, 34–35
Pemberton, Ebenezer, 46, 81
Penn, William, 103
Pennsylvania: assembly dispute
    with governor, 103, 105;
    assembly on English govern-
    ment, 87, 107; assembly and
    impeachment, 107–108; assembly
    on liberty, 126; assembly on tax
    power, 124; charter discussed,
    102, 103–104, 105–106,
    107–108; Quaker role in, 66, 68
Pennsylvania Gazette: on consti-
    tution, 50, 103–104; on press
    freedom, 28–29, 32; on religious
    tolerance, 63, 64
Pennsylvania Journal, 45, 121
*Pennsylvania Journal and
    Gazette,* 68–69
"Pennsylvanus," 106
Persecution, 62
Petition of Right, 97, 134
Philadelphia, 23, 25
"Philanthropos," 91
Philips, Samuel, 56
"Philo-Patriae," 50, 106
Plaintruth, Zacharius, 137
Plato, 84
"Plebeian," 45
Power: limits of, 81; locus of, 131
Presbyterianism, 133
Prince George's County, Md., 123

Printers: prosecution of, 21; role
    of, 23–24
Property and liberty, 43, 125
Puritans, 65–66

Quakers: and King George's War,
    66–68; orthodoxy of, 64, 68;
    persecuted in New England, 62
Quo Warranto, 133

Randolph, Sir John, 137–138
Rebellion, 38, 46, 49
Rhode Island, 63, 113
Robbins, Caroline, 16
Rome, 87
Rossiter, Clinton P., 12, 14
"Rusticus," 45, 57–58

Savelle, Max, 13
Seditious libel, 21, 27, 29, 31–34
Silence Dogood Letters, 23
Smith, Josiah, 62
Smith, William, 96–97, 120
Smith, Reverend William, 121
Smith, William, Jr., 73
South Carolina Gazette, 25
Spotswood, Alexander, 135
Stamp Act, 19, 145
Stevens, Benjamin, 59–60, 76
Submission, doctrine of, 81
Sydney, Algernon, 29

Taxation, 12, 118, 122, 123,
    124, 126
Thomas, George, 66–67
Timothy, Lewis, 25
Toleration, Act of, 61, 134
Toleration, religious, 63–64. *See
    also* Liberty of conscience.
Tory press, 21
Trenchard, John, 25

University of Washington, 161

Virginia, 135
"Virginia Centinel, No. XI," 93–94
Virginia Gazette, 32
Virginia, Governor of, 52

"Watchman," 45
"Watchtower," 32–34, 74, 121
Webbe, John: function of government, 88–91; limits on power, 82; press freedom, 30; religious toleration, 63–64; state of nature, 41
Welsteed, William, 56–57, 92
Willard, Samuel, 45–46, 80
William and Mary, 133
Williams, Abraham, 45, 60, 77
Williams, Elisha, 42–43, 52, 127

Williams, Roger, 12, 61
Winthrop, John, 76
Wise, Jeremiah, 51
Wise, John, 12, 40–41, 48
Woodward, John, 47
Wright, John, 120

"X.Z.," 71

"Z." *See* Webbe, John.
Zenger, John Peter, 24–25, 26, 27–28, 50, 87, 135

AMERICAN HISTORY TITLES IN THE NORTON LIBRARY

David Ammerman *In the Common Cause: American Response to the Coercive Acts of 1774* N787

Bernard Bailyn *Education in the Forming of American Society* N643

Samuel Flagg Bemis *John Quincy Adams and the Foundations of American Foreign Policy* N684

Samuel Flagg Bemis *The Latin American Policy of the United States* N412

Ray Allen Billington, Ed. *The Reinterpretation of Early American History* N446

Henry Blumenthal *France and the United States: Their Diplomatic Relations, 1789–1914* N625

T. H. Breen *The Character of the Good Ruler: Puritan Political Ideas in New England, 1630–1730* N747

Fawn Brodie *Thaddeus Stevens* N331

Robert E. Brown *Charles Beard and the Constitution* N296

Roger H. Brown *The Republic in Peril: 1812* N578

David Burner *The Politics of Provincialism: The Democratic Party in Transition, 1918–1932* N792

Richard L. Bushman *From Puritan to Yankee: Character and the Social Order in Connecticut, 1690–1765* N532

Stanley W. Campbell *The Slave Catchers: Enforcement of the Fugitive Slave Law, 1850–1860* N626

Mark Lincoln Chadwin *The Warhawks: American Interventionists Before Pearl Harbor* N546

Steven A. Channing *Crisis of Fear: Secession in South Carolina* N730

H. Trevor Colbourn *The Lamp of Experience: Whig History and the Intellectual Origins of the American Revolution* N714

Dudley T. Cornish *The Sable Arm: Negro Troops in the Union Army, 1861–1865* N334

Richard C. Cortner *The Apportionment Cases* N637

Robert F. Dalzell, Jr. *Daniel Webster and the Trial of American Nationalism, 1843–1852* N782

Philip Davidson *Propaganda and the American Revolution* N703

Dwight Lowell Dumond *Antislavery* N370

Richard S. Dunn *Puritans and Yankees: The Winthrop Dynasty of New England, 1630–1717* N597

Richard E. Ellis *The Jeffersonian Crisis: Courts and Politics in the Young Republic* N729

W. McKee Evans *Ballots and Fence Rails: Reconstruction on the Lower Cape Fear* N711

Federal Writers' Project *These Are Our Lives* N763

Herbert Feis *Contest Over Japan* N466

Herbert Feis *The Diplomacy of the Dollar* N333

Herbert Feis *The Spanish Story* N339

Herbert Feis *Three International Episodes: Seen from E. A.* N351

Robert H. Ferrell *American Diplomacy in the Great Depression: Hoover-Stimson Foreign Policy, 1929–1933* N511

Robert H. Ferrell *Peace in Their Time: The Origins of the Kellogg-Briand Pact* N491

John Hope Franklin *The Free Negro in North Carolina, 1790–1860* N579

Margaret Fuller *Woman in the Nineteenth Century* N615

Charles S. Grant *Democracy in the Connecticut Frontier Town of Kent* N639

Dewey W. Grantham *The Democratic South* N299

Fletcher Green *Constitutional Development in the South Atlantic States, 1776–1860* N348

Jack P. Greene *The Quest for Power: The Lower Houses of Assembly in the Southern Royal Colonies, 1689–1776* N591

Ira D. Gruber *The Howe Brothers and the American Revolution* N756

David D. Hall *The Faithful Shepherd: A History of the New England Ministry in the Seventeenth Century* N719

Michael Garibaldi Hall *Edward Randolph and the American Colonies, 1676–1703* N480

Holman Hamilton *Prologue to Conflict: The Crisis and Compromise of 1850* N345

Pendleton Herring *The Politics of Democracy* N306

Brooke Hindle *The Pursuit of Science in Revolutionary America, 1735–1789* N710

Robert V. Hine *California's Utopian Colonies* N678

Preston J. Hubbard *Origins of the TVA: The Muscle Shoals Controversy, 1920–1932* N467

Thomas Jefferson *Notes on the State of Virginia* N647

George F. Kennan *Realities of American Foreign Policy* N320

Gabriel Kolko *Railroads and Regulation, 1877–1916* N531

Benjamin W. Labaree *Patriots and Partisans: The Merchants of Newburyport, 1764–1815* N786

Howard Roberts Lamar *The Far Southwest, 1846–1912: A Territorial History* N522

Peggy Lamson *The Glorious Failure: Black Congressman Robert Brown Elliott and the Reconstruction in South Carolina* N733

William L. Langer *Our Vichy Gamble* N379

Douglas Edward Leach *Flintlock and Tomahawk: New England in King Philip's War* N340

William Letwin, Ed. *A Documentary History of American Economic Policy Since 1789* (Rev. Ed.) N442

Richard P. McCormick *The Second American Party System: Party Formation in the Jacksonian Era* N680

Forrest McDonald *The Presidency of George Washington* N773

William S. McFeely *Yankee Stepfather: General O. O. Howard and the Freedmen* N537

James Madison *Notes of Debates in the Federal Convention of 1787 Reported by James Madison* N485

C. Peter Magrath *Yazoo: The Case of Fletcher v. Peck* N418

Jackson Turner Main *The Antifederalists: Critics of the Constitution, 1781–1788* N760

Jackson Turner Main *Political Parties Before the Constitution* N718

Donald R. Matthews *U.S. Senators and Their World* (Rev. Ed.) N679

Burl Noggle *Teapot Dome* N297

Douglass C. North *The Economic Growth of the United States, 1790–1860* N346

Norman Pollack *The Populist Response to Industrial America* N295

Benjamin Quarles *The Negro in the American Revolution* N674

Robert E. Quirk *An Affair of Honor: Woodrow Wilson and the Occupation of Veracruz* N390

Robert E. Quirk *The Mexican Revolution, 1914–1915* N507

Robert V. Remini *Martin Van Buren and the Making of the Democratic Party* N527

Charles R. Ritcheson *Aftermath of Revolution: British Policy Toward the United States, 1783–1795* N553

Eric Robson *The American Revolution, In Its Political and Military Aspects, 1763–1783* N382

Darrett B. Rutman *Winthrop's Boston* N627

Bernard W. Sheehan *Seeds of Extinction: Jeffersonian Philanthropy and the American Indian* N715

James W. Silver *Confederate Morale and Church Propaganda* N422

Abbot E. Smith *Colonists in Bondage: White Servitude and Convict Labor in America, 1607–1776* N592

James Morton Smith, Ed. *Seventeenth-Century America* N629

Paul H. Smith *Loyalists and Redcoats: A Study in British Revolutionary Policy* N628

John W. Spanier *The Truman-MacArthur Controversy and the Korean War* N279

Julia Cherry Spruill *Women's Life and Work in the Southern Colonies* N662

Ralph Stone *The Irreconcilables: The Fight Against the League of Nations* N671

Ida M. Tarbell *History of the Standard Oil Company* (David Chalmers, Ed.) N496

George Brown Tindall *The Disruption of the Solid South* N663

Frederick B. Tolles *Meeting House and Counting House* N211

Arthur B. Tourtellot *Lexington and Concord* N194

Frederick Jackson Turner *The United States 1830–1850* N308

Richard W. Van Alstyne *The Rising American Empire* N750

Harris Gaylord Warren *Herbert Hoover and the Great Depression* N394

Wilcomb E. Washburn *The Governor and the Rebel: A History of Bacon's Rebellion in Virginia* N645

Thomas Tileston Waterman *The Dwellings of Colonial America* N646

John J. Waters, Jr. *The Otis Family in Provincial and Revolutionary Massachusetts* N759

John D. Weaver *The Brownsville Raid* N695

Arthur P. Whitaker *The United States and the Independence of Latin America* N271

Joel Williamson *After Slavery: The Negro in South Carolina During Reconstruction, 1861–1877* N759

Ola Elizabeth Winslow *Meetinghouse Hill, 1630–1783* N632

Bryce Wood *The Making of the Good Neighbor Policy* N401

Gordon S. Wood *The Creation of the American Republic, 1776–1787* N644

Peter H. Wood *Black Majority: Negroes in Colonial South Carolina from 1670 Through the Stono Rebellion* N777

Benjamin Fletcher Wright *Consensus and Continuity, 1776–1787* N402

Howard Zinn *LaGuardia in Congress* N488

Hiller B. Zobel *The Boston Massacre* N606